Gay & Lesbian

Parenting Choices

From Adopting or Using a Surrogate
to Choosing the Perfect Father

By Brette McWhorter Sember

CAREER
PRESS

Franklin Lakes, NJ

GAY & LESBIAN PARENTING CHOICES
EDITED AND TYPESET BY GINA TALUCCI
Cover design by Mada Design, Inc./NYC
Printed in the U.S.A. by Book-mart Press
Forms in this book from the Judicial Council of California
(*www.courtinfo.ca.gov*)
To order this title, please call toll-free 1-800-CAREER-1 (NJ and Canada: 201-848-0310) to order using VISA or MasterCard, or for further information on books from Career Press.

The Career Press, Inc., 3 Tice Road, PO Box 687,
Franklin Lakes, NJ 07417
www.careerpress.com

Library of Congress Cataloging-in-Publication Data

Sember, Brette McWhorter, 1968-
    Gay & lesbian parenting choices : from adoptions or using a surrogate to choosing the perfect father / by Brette McWhorter Sember
        p. cm.
    Includes bibliographical references and index.
    ISBN-13: 978-1-56414-837-7
        1. Gay adoption. 2. Gay parents. 3. Children of gay parents. 4. Surrogate mothers. 5. Fertilization in vitro. 6. Sperm banks. 7. Artificial insemination, Human. I. Title: Gay and lesbian parenting choices. II. Title.

HV875.715.S45 2006
362.82′8--dc22

2005058238

Acknowledgments

Many thanks go to my agent and friend Gina Panettieri for her insight, friendship, efforts, amazing ability, as well as the lottery tickets. This book would not exist without the amazing team at Career Press, who are always knowledgeable, professional, and friendly. As a writer I could not ask for better support. Personal thanks as always to my parents, husband, children, and friend Belle, who are with me every step of the journey.

Contents

Introduction

It is easier now than ever before for GLBTs (Gays, Lesbians, Bisexuals, and Transsexuals) to become parents. Becoming a parent is probably the most important thing you'll ever do, which I can attest to, as the mother of two children, and it's something everyone should have access to if they choose. This book is your guide to all the possibilities and choices before you. Whether you are interested in adopting a child, using a surrogate, finding a sperm donor, or being a foster parent, you have many avenues open to you. You will find that no matter what state you live in, there are a wide variety of options and there is no reason not to become a parent, if that is what you dream of.

Becoming a parent isn't as simple as sperm meeting egg for most gay singles or couples, and often there is the added hurdle of going through a second parent adoption to make sure your partner (if you have one) can also become a legal parent. Without question though, any legal steps you need to take will be well worth it once you hold your own child in your arms, and this book will help guide you through the steps you need to take to make that happen.

Because laws about adoption and assisted fertility are changing frequently (and mostly for the good), it's always a good idea to consult with an attorney in your state to get the most up-to-date information available. Additionally, forms in each state will differ, so it's essential to make sure you use the correct documents for your state, which an attorney can provide you with.

This publication is designed to provide accurate and authoritative information in regard to the subject matter covered. It is sold with the understanding that the publisher or author is not engaged in rendering legal, accounting , or other professional services. If legal advice or other expert assistance is required, the services of a competent professional person should be sought. This book is not a substitute for legal advice. All forms in the book are for the purposes of example only.

My wish for you is your dream family, and I hope this book helps make it happen.

Chapter 1

Deciding to Become a Parent

Deciding to become a parent is an exciting time. You've decided that you want to become a family—whether you will be a single parent or a parent with a partner. For many heterosexuals, deciding to have a family is a pretty easy process, but for GLBT singles or couples, it's a complicated matter. This isn't something you can do completely on your own and you have to involve other people in your procreation decision.

If you wish to become a parent, you will not be alone. It is estimated that there are more than 1 million children being raised in the United States by same sex parents, and this number does not include the many, many children being raised by gay singles. One in five male couples and one in three female couples had children in 2000.

The decision to become a parent is a crucial one, but once you've made that very important decision, you have a lot more decisions ahead of you. Each decision you make will bring you closer to your child, so it is a path most definitely worth walking.

Examine Your Legal Status

If you have a partner, it's important that you take a moment and consider your legal status towards each other. Becoming gay or lesbian parents is complicated and there are some steps you can take now that will make things easier for you down the road.

If you live in a state where gay marriage or civil unions are legal, you may be better off if you legalized your relationship. In these states, doing so will mean that you can both become legal parents at the same moment, instead of having to deal with second parent adoption. It also will give you access to each other's health insurance and provide a lot of property protections that will be important for your new family. If you're opposed to marriage or insulted by civil unions, consider the important benefits this silly piece of paper can make for your child. He or she will be the legal child of both of you immediately and neither one of you will be given greater parental status than the other. This is an important benefit and one you should not dismiss lightly. If you're not impressed by that, consider the financial benefit. Getting married is cheap if you do it no frills, but paying an attorney to handle a second parent adoption is expensive—why waste the money when you can say "I do" and have it taken care of?

Deciding How to Become a Parent

You have two basic avenues to choose from if you want to become a parent. You can adopt a child or you can use assisted reproduction to create a child. Some people or couples know instantly which option is best for them, although others need to give it some thought. If you aren't sure which direction you want to go in, ask yourself these questions:

- ◪ Do you or your partner want to be biologically related to the child? If so, you'll want to use assisted reproduction.

- ◪ Would you be comfortable raising a child from another country or one who is of a different race or ethnicity? If so, you are a good candidate for international adoption or domestic adoption.

- ◪ Do you want to begin parenting when your child is an infant? If so, you will want to consider assisted reproduction and examine your options about adopting a newborn.

- ◪ How willing are you or your partner to undergo medical procedures and tests in the hopes of building a family, should that become necessary? If you are not, assisted reproduction may not work for you.

- ◪ How much money do you have available to spend on family building? See the following information to understand costs.

Approximate Costs of Assisted Fertility vs. Adoption

Fertility treatments

- ◪ Donor Insemination: $500 per cycle

- ◪ Egg Donation: $7,500 per cycle

- Embryo Donation: $3,000 per cycle

- Surrogacy: $25,000 to $50,000

Adoption procedures

- Foster care adoption: $2,500

- Domestic agency adoption: $4,000 to $30,000

- International adoption: $10,000 to $40,000

- Domestic parent-facilitated or independent adoptions $8,000 to $30,000

Both of the options have benefits and drawbacks, so take a moment and weigh them.

Assisted Fertility

Pros

- You can create a child who is related to you or your partner.

- If you are lesbians, one of you can carry the pregnancy and give birth to the baby.

- If you are lesbians, you may be able to conceive quickly and with minimum intervention.

- The donor or surrogate you use will have no ongoing role in your child's life. You will have no obligation to him or her, unless you choose to specifically involve him or her.

◪ You have flexibility for your family. You can create your own expanded family by making donors or surrogates honorary aunts or uncles in your child's life, and you follow your own timeline for the creation of your family.

◪ There are no court procedures to go through. However, if you choose surrogacy, there are court procedures.

◪ If you use home insemination, you don't need to rely on anyone to create your family.

Cons

◪ Timing is everything. If you use donor sperm, you may need to manage your cycle to optimize your chances for getting pregnant and may need to chart your temperature or use ovulation kits.

◪ You have the burden of selecting your child's other biological parent. This can be a difficult decision.

◪ There are no refunds. You pay for procedures whether they are successful or not.

◪ Fertility costs can be greater than adoption costs, if you do a lot of cycles or have to try many different procedures.

◪ There are entanglements. If you use a known donor or surrogate, you do have to deal with interpersonal relationships with him or her and you may have differing expectations.

Adoption

Pros

- ◪ You can be almost certain that a child will be placed with you, depending on the type of adoption you choose.

- ◪ The costs for an adoption are more fixed than they are for fertility procedures so you can know in advance how much money you will need to create your family.

- ◪ You may be able to see or meet your child before you make the final decision to adopt him.

- ◪ You do not have to go through the agonizing waiting process each month of finding out if you're pregnant.

- ◪ You know that you've done something wonderful for a child who needs a home.

Cons

- ◪ It is very unlikely that you will be able to adopt a newborn.

- ◪ If you adopt internationally you may have very little information about your child's family history and medical background.

- ◪ The birth parents may want to meet you and have ongoing contact with your child. This can be complicated for everyone involved.

◪ Other people will evaluate you and not all will be gay-friendly. You must pass a home study in order to be allowed to adopt and you must go through a court process to legally adopt your child.

◪ It is more expensive to pay for an adoption than it is to pay for one or two less invasive fertility procedures. This is a balancing of odds though. You might take five cycles to get pregnant, or you might need only one.

Deciding Who Will Be the Biological Parent

If you have a partner and you want to use assisted reproduction, only one of you can be the child's biological parent. If you are lesbians, it is possible to use one parent's eggs and the other parent's uterus, so this is an option you can consider that allows both of you to participate in the pregnancy. If you choose this option, you will need to use a fertility clinic and there will be more expenses than if you use only donor insemination.

If you are gay men, you don't necessarily have to decide who will be the father. A mix of both your sperm can be used to inseminate the eggs and you could choose to never find out which one of you is the biological father.

Note that if you choose adoption and one of you has HIV, it will be simplest for the other partner to adopt first, with the HIV-infected partner becoming a parent by a late second parent adoption process because health is an issue in adoptions.

Arranging Your Finances

When anyone chooses to have a child, it brings with it new costs and financial responsibilities. Adoption and assisted reproduction bring added costs to the family building process. Once you've decided what avenue you want to take to have a child, you need to consider how you will afford the costs.

You may have savings you can use, or you may be able to adjust your spending so that you have funds available. If you are using assisted reproduction, find out what payment options your clinic has available—many have payment plans available that can make the process easier.

If you are considering adoption, you'll need to think about the varying costs of different types of adoptions. International adoptions are the most expensive, and domestic public agency adoptions are the least expensive. Your employer may offer adoption expense reimbursement and you will also qualify for a tax credit with the federal government if you adopt. You can also apply for special adoption assistance loans.

If you are creating a family with a partner, this is also the time to consider your health insurance options. If you each have your own health insurance policies, you need to compare them to determine which offers the most favorable family policy. Consider copays, deductibles, referral requirements, prescription costs, coinsurance costs, as well as coverage and participating providers. Once you have a child, you will want to place the child on the policy that offers the best deal. If you are permitted to, you will probably want to include your partner on that policy as well.

Chapter 2

Your Adoption Choices

If you're considering adoption, you know there are a variety of different adoption options you can consider. You can adopt a child from another country, or one from this country. You can adopt a child using an agency, or without an agency's help. You can adopt through a private adoption agency or a public one. You can adopt a baby, a toddler, or an older child. There are a lot of choices, and it can be difficult to decide what the best direction is.

Adopting as a Single or a Couple

If you are single and wish to adopt, being gay is not a barrier. Although Florida does not permit adoptions by gay people and other countries do not permit adoption by gays, for the most part, if you don't offer information about your sexuality, no one will know (and no one will ask). What is important to remember is that if you are asked, you should be honest, but for the most part there is no need to come out and tell anyone you are working with or that you are gay or lesbian.

> You can learn about how suited you are for adoption by taking the adoption self-assessment at *http://adoption.about.com/library/adopt/blselfeval.htm*.

If you and a partner wish to adopt a child together, you need to determine your state's laws about same sex couple adoption. In the following states you can adopt a child together in a one step process: Vermont, New Jersey, California, Connecticut, Illinois, New Mexico, New York, Oregon, District of Columbia, and Massachusetts (at the time this book was published, Massachusetts has legal marriages for same sex couples, thus allowing same sex couple adoption by married couples, but a large movement was underway to attempt to reverse the Massachusetts marriage law, so be sure to check for current developments).

If your state does not permit adoption by a same-sex couple, you and your partner can still adopt using a two step process called "second parent adoption." This is the same procedure that is used to allow a stepparent to adopt a child in a straight couple. For information about second parent adoption, see Chapter 4.

> Join an online gay adoption support group at *www.cyberhiway.com/aparent/faq.html*.

Transgender Adoption

There are no laws that prevent transgender people from adopting, although you can expect to encounter a lot of ignorance and resistance. If you are transgender and would like to adopt, work only with an agency that is known for being gay-friendly. Make sure that you have a physician and a mental health worker who are willing to talk to the social worker or agency personnel about transgender situations. It's also essential to work with an attorney who is experienced in transgender issues, even if he or she only consults on the case with your adoption attorney.

Open or Closed Adoption

Adoption used to be something that was done in secrecy and many children grew up without ever knowing they were adopted. Fortunately, this has changed and almost all adoptive children are now told they were adopted. An open adoption simply means that the adoptive and birth parents have some contact. The amount of contact can vary greatly though. Some adoptive parents make the birth parents part of their extended family, while others simply are able to tell their child the name of the birth mother and where she lived and have her family medical history.

Open adoption is not always possible. International adoptions often provide no contact with birth parents, but you may be able to obtain family medical history and the birth mother's name in some situations. Private adoptions can be some of the most open adoptions, and domestic agency adoptions can vary greatly depending on the agency's policies, your wishes, and the birth mother's wishes.

Open adoption agreements are not documents that are legally enforceable by a court, but they can provide a helpful blueprint so that everyone involved understands exactly how the relationship will progress and be structured.

Choosing an open or closed adoption depends on your personal feelings. It's important to understand that your adoption won't be specified as open or closed in your adoption papers. The court cannot require you to send photos to the birth mother, but it can't prevent you from having a relationship with her either. As far as the court is concerned, the adoptive parent(s) becomes the legal parent(s) and the birth parent(s) has/have no further rights once the adoption is completed. The adoption legal process completely ends the birth parents' legal rights, but anything you choose to do from that point is up to you. However, it's important to realize that some birth mothers will not agree to the adoption if they don't feel you have made a commitment to the level of openness (or closure) they are seeking.

> For more information about open adoption, contact the American Association of Open Adoption Agencies at *www.openadoption.org* or see *Open Adoption Experience: Complete Guide for Adoptive and Birth Families* by Lois Ruskai Melina.

Domestic or International Adoption

Deciding whether to adopt a child from the United States or from another country is a difficult decision. There are pros and cons to both options, and when it comes right down to it, the decision needs to be based on what you (and your partner if you have one) feel most comfortable with. Consider the following when making this decision:

Domestic Adoption

Pros

- ◪ You may be able to adopt a newborn. International adoptions usually do not occur until late infancy or after because of the waiting periods imposed by the countries the children are from. If you really want to adopt a newborn, a domestic adoption is the only way to ensure this.

- ◪ You will obtain your child's complete family medical history. This is not always possible in international adoptions where the child may be an orphan and existing health records may not be easily obtainable.

- ◪ Everything is conducted in English. If you adopt internationally, you will have a language barrier and will need to rely on others to help you deal with that.

- ◪ You can have contact with the birth parents. If they wish to have contact, you can get to know them and possibly keep in touch with them if you wish.

- ◪ You may only have to work with one agency. The child you adopt may be placed for adoption with the agency you apply to and this greatly simplifies things.

- ◪ The adoption is done using clear U.S. adoption laws. International adoptions are known for delays and inexplicable bureaucracy problems. If you adopt domestically, waiting periods and procedures are clear cut.

- You child has the possibility of one day finding and meeting her birth parents. In international adoptions, this is unlikely.

Cons

- It can take a year or longer to have a child placed with you. International adoptions generally do not take as long to have a child available.

- If you want a newborn, you may have to wait even longer.

- You always have the possibility of a birth mother or father who could change his or her mind after the baby is born and decide not to go through with the adoption. In international adoptions, the child is usually not placed until she is completely freed for adoption.

- Birth mothers have the ultimate decision and may be choosy or indecisive about the family they want their child placed with. In international adoptions, birth parents have no control over placement.

International Adoption

Pros

- International adoptions happen more quickly than domestic adoptions. If you are anxious to have a child soon, this option may appeal to you.

- There is no shortage of children available. In the United States the only children that are widely available for adoption immediately are older children who have gone through foster care.

◪ International adoptions are less expensive than domestic adoptions.

◪ Your child brings his or her culture to your family.

Cons

◪ Newborns are not available for adoption.

◪ Children may have health problems. It is not uncommon for children from other countries to experience illnesses and developmental delays that are uncommon in the United States.

◪ Medical information may not be available. You may get a family health history, but it is unlikely. At the very least you will get what health records are available for any care your child has received at the facility he is staying at.

◪ You may need to travel to meet requirements for the adoption.

◪ You may encounter red tape. The adoption process and government officials are very different in other countries and the process can take longer than anticipated with last-minute delays.

◪ You will need to adopt your child in her country of origin and then also do a U.S. adoption to make sure it is official.

Agency or Private Adoption

An agency adoption is one in which you sign on with an adoption agency that locates a child for you to adopt. The agency provides a social worker to do your home study and also provides counseling and other services along the way. In a private adoption, you locate a birth mother on your own: through adoption attorneys, adoption facilitators, word of mouth, or by placing newspaper ads. However, many adoptive parents who do private adoptions use an agency to handle the adoption once the birth mother is located. The agency provides the home study if one has not been completed and manages the adoption process.

Agency Adoption

Pros

- ◪ The agency locates and places the child with you. You don't have to do the legwork.

- ◪ The agency manages the adoption. They provide a social worker who will do your home study, as well as counseling and services. In short, this is one-stop shopping.

- ◪ A good agency has many children available. This increases your chance of having a child placed with you quickly.

- ◪ The agency provides a buffer. You, as well as the birth parents, can come to them for help. The agency also has experience working with birth parents.

- ◪ The agency screens birth parents. They are able to eliminate those who are most likely to change their minds.

- ◪ The agency can place a child more quickly. It has a network in place to locate birth mothers.

Cons

- ◪ You are dealing with a bureaucratic agency. Things may move slowly because of the procedures that are in place.

- ◪ The agency screens potential parents. You may find that some agencies funded by churches are not as friendly to gays as others might be.

- ◪ The agency is in control of your adoption. You must rely on them completely to handle it for you.

- ◪ It may cost more. You pay agency fees in addition to the other adoption costs.

Private Adoptions

Pros

- ◪ You are completely in control of the entire process.

- ◪ Your relationship with the birth mother develops at the pace you set.

- ◪ You find and select the birth mother.

- ◪ You have the opportunity to gather as much information as you would like about the birth parents.

- ◪ Fewer people are involved with your adoption.

- ◪ You can bond with the child from birth, instead of waiting for placement to occur.

- ◪ You do not need to worry about finding an agency that is gay-friendly.

Cons

- ◪ You are inexperienced at handling adoptions. This means you may make mistakes.

- ◪ The process is riskier. The birth mother may be more likely to change her mind. You don't have a lot of backup or people to help you keep it on track.

- ◪ The burden is on you to find a birth mother. It is your responsibility (and your expense) to advertise and search for birth mothers.

- ◪ You don't have experts guiding you. You must understand your state's laws and find an experienced attorney to represent you as you search for birth mothers.

- ◪ You can't choose the child's gender. You contract with the birth mother before the child is born and whatever she has, you adopt. If you use an agency, you can specify the gender you want to adopt.

- ◪ Costs are more unpredictable. You don't have an agency following a set procedure.

- ◪ It may be more stressful. When you don't use an agency, more of the responsibility rests on you.

Finding and Choosing an Attorney

No matter what type of adoption you are interested in, you will need an attorney to represent you. It's important to choose an attorney who is experienced in handling adoptions, and particularly one who has worked with gay couples in the past.

If you have an attorney you have used for other matters, ask her for a referral. Ask members of your adoption support group for referrals. Talk to acquaintances and check online discussion boards for recommendations. You can also call your state or city bar association and ask for a referral. Your local pride or advocacy group may also be of assistance.

Once you have some attorneys to consider, schedule a free consultation with each. Use the Attorney Questionnaire later in this section to help you evaluate the attorneys you meet with. Make sure you get a clear picture of the attorney's fees. If you are seeking a private adoption, you will need to find out if the attorney is able to help you locate birth mothers or if he will only handle the legal paperwork.

Expect attorney fees to range from $2,000 to $6,000, depending on the type of adoption and where you live. If you will be doing a second parent adoption, you will incur additional fees for that. Avoid attorneys who seek contingency fees. These attorneys are paid only if they accomplish certain things (such as finding a child for you to adopt). Make sure that when you do select an attorney that your agreement with her is written and is in the form of a retainer agreement or retainer letter.

Attorney Evaluation Questionnaire

Name of Firm

Name of Attorney

Date of Interview

Questions:

1. How long have you practiced adoption law?
2. How many adoptions do you handle per year?
3. How many adoptions do you handle per year for gay singles or couples?
4. Do you handle domestic or international adoptions or both?

5. Do you handle private adoptions? How many have you handled? What role do you take in the private adoption process?

6. What are your fees? Do you charge a flat fee or an hourly rate? Are there additional fees for second parent adoptions?

7. Can you recommend any agencies that you have worked with in the past?

8. How long does the average adoption process take?

9. What kind of adoption is possible in our state—joint, second parent, or only single adoptions?

Facilitators

Adoption facilitators are professionals who locate birth mothers for adoptive parents. They can play an ongoing role throughout the adoption process and take on a coordinating position similar to an agency. Be aware that many states do not permit the use of adoption facilitators. Some states do permit facilitators to operate, but do not license or regulate them. California does license facilitators. Be sure to talk to your attorney about the legalities of using a facilitator and also be certain to check references and backgrounds of any facilitators you consider. Don't work with anyone without a contract and make sure that your attorney approves the contract. It is very important that you only work with a facilitator who has successfully placed many adoptions.

Nonfacilitator Private Adoptions

If you don't want to do an agency adoption, you can still do a private adoption without a facilitator if they are illegal in your state, or you don't want to work with one. It's essential that you work with an experienced attorney who can guide you through the process. Some attorneys function similar to facilitators and have contacts that can help you locate a birth mother. Just be sure that any attorney you work with has successfully completed many adoptions and has experience working with gay adoptive parents. See Chapter 7 for more information about independent adoptions.

> Information to help you consider domestic versus international adoption is available at: *www.adoptall.com/intguide.html.*

One of the most comprehensive and helpful resources available to parents seeking to adopt is the National Adoption Information Clearinghouse at *www.calib.com/naic.* This site is almost certain to provide answers to almost any question you have.

For a referral to an attorney, contact: American Academy of Adoption Attorneys, *www.adoptionattorneys.org.*

Chapter 3

The Adoption Process

The most important thing to remember about an adoption is that although it is an important emotional process, it is first and foremost a legal process. And this means there are hoops to jump through and requirements to meet, as well as waiting periods to cope with. Take things one step at a time and you will make it through the process, no matter how lengthy it might seem to you at times. There are plenty of children available for adoption, so you feel confident that you will become a parent.

Choosing an Adoption Agency

If you choose to work with an agency to adopt, you should interview several agencies and choose the one that you are most comfortable with and confident in. Adoption is expensive and you want to be sure you choose an agency who will give you what you're paying for. Agencies can be profit or non-profit, but they all have fees. Agencies can be public (run by the state) or private (run by a private company), with private agencies being more expensive. Agencies can also be religious or nonsectarian, but it is important to know that most religious-based agencies do not require adoptive parents to be members of that religion, although it may be more difficult for gay parents to adopt.

A study by the Evan B. Donaldson Adoption Institute showed that 60 percent of adoption agencies allowed gays to adopt, but public agencies were more gay-friendly than private agencies. An agency cannot reject you because of race or religion, but marital status and sexual orientation *can* be used as criteria, unfortunately.

The best way to locate an agency is by word of mouth, through adoption support groups, or people you know who have used an agency successfully. Once you have a few agencies to consider, make an initial phone call and request information by mail. Here are a few other things to consider:

- ☑ Ask point blank if they have worked with gay couples successfully. If you are a gay single, ask if they work with single gay parents.

- ☑ If you are planning on not revealing that you are gay, be sure to just make an anonymous call.

- ☑ If the agency has a Website, visit it to find out more information.

- ☑ Don't sign up with any agency before you've had time to ask questions, compare it to others, and think about the decision.

- ☑ Ask about informational meetings and be sure to attend them.

- ☑ Ask questions and be observant.

- ☑ Go up at the end of the meeting and talk to the representatives from the agency. If you sense hostility, this might not be the agency for you.

- ☑ If you still feel the agency is a possibility, schedule an interview and use the questionnaire at the end of this section as an organizing tool.

The agency's fee will be an important consideration for you. The agency charges fees to cover the home study, application, birth mother's expenses (if it is a domestic private adoption), and other costs. Some agencies will clearly enunciate these separate amounts for you. Be wary of an agency that lumps total costs together and will not provide a break down.

Call your state agency that licenses and monitors adoption agencies (your social services or family and children department) and ask for information about the agency, including its history and any complaints that have been filed against it. Ask to speak to an adoption specialist in the department and ask about the agency's reputation. If you're considering a public agency, realize that you can't really get an objective evaluation of the agency when talking to other state employees.

The average length of time for a domestic private adoption should be less than two years. If an agency has a longer average, you might want to go somewhere else.

When you decide to use an agency, make sure you get everything in writing so that there can be no confusion or dispute. You will need to sign a contract with the agency that will spell out fees, procedures, and responsibilities.

Agency Evaluation Questionnaire

Name of Agency

Name of Contact Person

Date of interview

Questions:

1. Are you licensed in this state?
2. How long have you been in business?
3. Can you provide references?
4. Do you handle domestic or international adoptions? If both, which do you place more often?
5. Can you place children from other states?
6. Do you have religious restrictions?
7. What other guidelines or restrictions do you have in place?
8. What is your fee structure? Can you provide a breakdown? When are the amounts due? What fees are not included in this?
9. What is the average length of time for one of your adoptions?
10. How many placements do you make per year? How many in the last year?
11. How many people are on the waiting list to adopt?
12. Do you have infants available? What is the average age of children placed through your agency?
13. What portion of your fees are refundable if the adoption does succeed?
14. Please explain your home study process. How long does it take?
15. Can you provide a list of approved social workers to use for the home study?
16. Will you assist with a private adoption? What fees would apply?

17. How are your birth mothers located and screened?

18. Who makes the placement decision—the agency or the birth mother? How is placement decided?

19. What is your position on open adoption? What kind of relationship do you encourage or advise birth parents and adoptive parents to have?

20. Do you provide counseling for birth and adoptive parents? Is it mandatory? Are there additional fees for this? What is involved in the counseling process?

21. What medical history information is provided to adoptive parents about the birth parents? Are birth mothers screened for HIV and other conditions?

22. If a potential adoptive parent turns down a birth mother, may they continue in the program and receive the next available placement?

23. If an adoption is not completed, can the expenses paid be transferred or rolled over to a new birth mother?

24. What other services does the agency provide?

25. What is your policy on divorce, singles, gays, and families with biological children?

26. Do you have a grievance policy? If so how does it work? If not, how are problems resolved?

Affording Adoption

When considering adoption, many people are taken aback by the costs involved. But adoption is not always as expensive as it might seem. If you choose to adopt a child out of foster care, the state may take on most or all of the fees, making this a very affordable way to adopt.

In addition, there are ways to make private agency adoption more affordable. You may wish to consider purchasing adoption insurance, which will reimburse you for expenses if a planned adoption does not take place. There are also special low-interest loans available to prospective adoptive parents. For more information about adoption insurance and loans, contact: National Adoption Foundation at *www.nafadopt.org.* The National Endowment for Financial Education offers helpful information about affording adoption at *www.nefe.org/adoption/.* Once you adopt, you're entitled to up to a $10,000 federal tax deduction for the expenses associated with your adoption that you have not been reimbursed for. If you adopt a special needs child, you are entitled to the full deduction (with some income restrictions) without having to show expenses. Additionally, if you can't take the full deduction, you can carry forward (take in later years) the remaining amounts. Talk to your accountant or tax preparer about this credit. Second parent adoptions do not qualify.

Additionally, once your child has been adopted, you can list him as a dependant on your taxes, so make sure you let your tax preparer know about the adoption. Some states also offer adoption tax credits, so inquire about this.

Many employers offer adoption expense reimbursement (a 2004 survey found that 39 percent of the top 936 U.S. employers provided some kind of assistance). Check with your human resource manager to find out if your company offers such a program. Most employers offer a lump sum payment between $1,000 and $15,000. Other employees pay for specific adoption expenses, such as agency or legal fees. You can view a list of employers who offer adoption benefits at *www.adoptionfriendlyworkplace.org/employers.asp*

Home Studies

Once you've selected an agency (if you will be working with an agency) and signed up with them, the next important step is a home study. A home study is an evaluation and investigation of prospective parents' histories, parenting abilities, home, lifestyle, and parenting plans, that is done by a social worker. Your sexual orientation will not necessarily come up, but if you live with a partner, it is likely that the worker will ask about what kind of relationship you have. Don't lie, but it is your choice whether to reveal that you are gay.

A home study will go into past addiction history and treatment (the GLBT community has a higher rate of addiction), and addiction can be a reason to deny an adoption. For lesbians with this type of problem, note that no home study is required if you use insemination to carry a child yourself, so this might be an alternative to consider.

Home studies are required in almost all adoptions, but in some states they may be waived for second parent adoptions. If you do an adoption and then do a second parent adoption where you need a home study, be sure to use the same social worker for both because it will make the process much simpler.

The agency may have a list of social workers it works with or may have social workers who are employed at the agency that will perform the study, however, you can find one on your own if you wish. Make sure that the social worker you use is licensed in your state.

The home study is probably the most feared hurdle in the adoption process by many prospective gay parents, but in reality, it is not nearly as terrifying as it may sound. Remember that what everyone in the system wants is to be able to place children with parents who will love them. The social worker wants to make sure that you're able to care for a child. Being an ax murderer is a no-no, but being gay is not a crime.

See a sample adoption home study online at *www.1-800-homestudy.com/homestudy/sample.*

A social worker will come to your home, meet you and your partner (if you have one), and ask you questions about your background. If you are acting as if your partner is merely a roommate and you are not disclosing that you are partners, you should make two bedrooms appear lived in with clothing and personal items and perhaps put away any photos of the two of you hugging, along with anything else in the house that suggests being gay or lesbian. Even if you pretend your partner is a roommate, the social worker will need to interview her—anyone who will live in the home with the child needs to be interviewed. And be aware that social workers are a perceptive sort, so it may be difficult to hide your relationship. The background questions you'll be asked include topics such as:

- ☑ where you were born

- ☑ your family

- ☑ your education

- ☑ your job history

- ☑ previous marriages (remember they're probably assuming you're straight)

- ☑ previous addresses

- ☑ any arrests or convictions

- ☑ information about children you have

The social worker will also ask questions about your lifestyle and personal life including:

- ☑ your employment schedule (to understand when you would have time for a child)

- ☑ income

- friends and family you spend time with (to get a picture of your support system)

- organizations you belong to

- pets

- religious beliefs and churches, temples, or mosques you belong to

- hobbies and interests, and how a child would fit in

- smoking, drinking, and drug use

- medical conditions (anything that might impair your ability to parent)

- how you plan to make room in your life for a child

- where the child will sleep

- childcare plans (such as daycare, a nanny, or a sitter)

- how you will discipline a child

- how you will adjust your finances to include a child

- any assisted reproduction treatments you have undergone or are undergoing. Some couples try insemination or surrogacy prior to, or while beginning, the adoption process. If you're the partner who has been inseminated, or if you're a gay man who has tried surrogacy, it's okay to discuss it. But unless being gay is something you are open about, don't mention your partner being inseminated or using a surrogate together.

The social worker will want to see your home and will be particularly interested in where the child will sleep. You do not need to have a nursery or bedroom all made up and ready for a child. You just need to be able to show you have a room that will work and demonstrate that you plan to childproof. Your home doesn't have to be spotless and it doesn't have to look similar to your typical middle-class family home. It just needs to be clear that a child would fit in there.

You may need to meet with the social worker more than once to cover all the information that is needed. Don't become overwhelmed by this process. Some prospective parents spend weeks repainting the house and decorating a nursery. Your home should simply be clean and neat. This isn't a contest to decide who would be the best parent. The home study is simply a way of making sure you're decent people who are able to care for a child.

Additionally you will be asked to write an autobiographical statement that really just restates the information you'll give to the social worker during your meetings. This statement is brief—just a page or two that includes information about why you want to adopt, as well as a brief history of your life. You will need to provide certified copies of birth and marriage certificates (if you were ever married, as well as divorce decrees, but you should refrain from providing certificates of domestic partnership unless being gay is not going to be a problem), and a medical report from your physician describing your health and explaining any conditions you have. You also need written proof of your income (pay stubs or tax returns).

Another part of the home study is providing references. You need three to five people who know you well to write letters and say nice things about you. Use a variety of people such as friends, neighbors, clergy, coworkers, and so on. They will be asked to explain how they know you, how long they have known you, and why they believe you would make good adoptive parents.

You will also need to be fingerprinted and/or have a criminal background check done. If your state requires fingerprints, you will be given a card or paperwork and told to go to your local police station to be fingerprinted. A background check requires you to complete a form with your name, address, and Social Security number. This is then run through a computer to check for convictions, child abuse problems, or outstanding warrants.

There is generally a separate fee for the home study that can range from $700 to $2,000, or a bit more. If you are working with an agency, this may not be included in the agency fees. Once the investigation has been completed, the social worker will write up a report that describes you and includes a recommendation as to whether you should adopt. The entire home study process can take anywhere from a few weeks to a few months, depending how quickly things can be scheduled and how soon you get the needed paperwork in.

Be sure to ask for a copy of the home study. It will be valid for a year to 18 months and should you switch agencies or change your plan, you won't want to have it redone. If your adoption isn't completed in that time frame, you might need to have it updated—a shorter and less expensive process.

Consent

All adoptions involve some form of consent—an agreement by the birth parents that the child can be adopted. If there are no living birth parents or the child was abandoned, then consent is given by the state or country the child is a resident of. Consent is the biggest and most important hurdle to adoption, and the legal procedures are in place to make sure birth parents are given adequate time to make the decision. You want to make sure the consent to your adoption is completely legal, because if it isn't, that's how problems arise after the fact. If you're working with an agency, this usually isn't a problem, but if you're doing a private adoption, it's essential that you work with an attorney who is experienced in handling this type of adoption and who will make sure that the consent to your adoption is bulletproof.

The birth mother must always provide consent to the adoption. The birth father must also provide consent, but only if paternity has been established. Paternity can be established through a formal legal admission by the father or through a court proceeding in which paternity is proven. Many states also have what is called a putative father registry. This is a place where a man can register if he believes he is the father of a child. Before a child is placed for adoption, the putative father registry must be searched. If someone has registered, paternity will be tested. The following states have putative father registries: Alabama, Arizona, Georgia, Idaho, Illinois, Indiana, Iowa, Kansas, Kentucky, Louisiana, Massachusetts, Minnesota, Missouri, New Mexico, New York, Ohio, Oklahoma, Oregon, South Dakota, Tennessee, Texas, Utah, Vermont, Wisconsin, and Wyoming.

No Consent Needed

Consent is not needed if the parent has abandoned the child, had his or her rights terminated by the state (usually through an abuse or neglect proceeding), is dead, or if there are special circumstances, such as failure of the parent to have contact with the child for a lengthy period of time.

Consent by the Child

In most states, older children who are adopted must give their consent (this normally comes into play when a child is adopted out of foster care). The age of consent varies:

- ☑ Age 10: Alaska, Arkansas, Hawaii, Maryland, New Jersey, New Mexico, and North Dakota.

- ☑ Age 12: Arizona, California, Colorado, Connecticut, Florida, Idaho, Kentucky, Massachusetts, Montana, New Hampshire, North Carolina, Ohio, Oklahoma, Pennsylvania, South Dakota, Texas, Utah, and West Virginia.

- ☑ Age 14: Alabama, Delaware, District of Columbia, Georgia, Illinois, Indiana, Iowa, Kansas, Maine, Michigan, Minnesota, Mississippi, Missouri, Nebraska, Nevada, New York, Oregon, Rhode Island, South Carolina, Vermont, Virginia, Washington, Wyoming

- ☑ Consent not required: Louisiana, Tennessee, and Wisconsin.

Notice

Often the birth father may not be part of the child's life, or may not be able to be located to give consent. When this happens, the court will allow legal notice to be given to him and if there is no response, no consent is necessary. Legal notice is specified in your state's laws and can include sending certified letters or court documents to his last known address or workplace, or publishing a notice in a newspaper selected by the court. If the father does not respond, he is presumed to have waived his right to oppose the adoption. If notice is required in your adoption, your attorney will take careful steps to make sure it is done correctly. If notice is not given properly, the birth father could later come back and seek custody, so this is a crucial part of the process. It's important to remember that thousands of adoptions take place every year with a notice component and nothing goes wrong, so try not to worry about it if notice has to be given in your case.

Timing of Consent

Birth fathers can give consent to adoption at any time, however there are specific time frames in which a birth mother must consent in order for the adoption to be legal. Formal, legal consent is usually required after the birth of the child although Alabama and Hawaii do allow consent beforehand, but require a reaffirmation after the birth. There is usually a waiting period between the birth and when the birth mother's consent becomes final, which can vary from 12 hours after the birth to 15 days afterwards.

Consent Procedures

Birth parent consent can be done in writing (usually notarized) in some states. Other states require that it be done in court— either by appearing before the judge or by filing certain court papers. The birth parent must indicate that he or she understands the ramifications and willingly gives up all rights to the child. Your attorney will explain the requirements in your state. Remember that obtaining consent and all the legal documentation is not your responsibility and will be handled by the agency and your attorney. You should feel free to ask questions about how the process will proceed and get details on when consent has to happen so that you know what to expect.

Revocation

Revocation is the legal withdrawal of consent by a birth parent who previously gave legal consent (note that this is different from a mother changing her mind and deciding after the birth that she doesn't want to place the baby for adoption—

that happens before consent has been finalized). You've probably heard horror stories about adoptions being revoked at the last minute. Revocation is actually difficult to do. A few states do not allow any revocation under any circumstances. Others permit revocation only if there has been fraud, coercion, or other factors that show the birth parent did not have complete knowledge of the adoption or free will at the time of the consent. A few states allow birth parents to change their minds for any reason within a certain time period, but this can only happen within a certain period of time, so there's no possibility of a birth mother coming back a year later and saying she wants her baby back.

Once the court has completely finalized the adoption (see later in this section for information on court proceedings), there is no possibility that the adoption can be revoked.

Time Period After Consent for Revocation

- ◪ No revocation allowed unless fraud, duress, and so on: Arizona, California (agency adoption), Colorado, Florida (if adoptive parents are identified), Kansas, Mississippi, Nebraska, New Hampshire, New Jersey, New Mexico, Oklahoma, Oregon, South Carolina, Utah, West Virginia, Wisconsin, and Wyoming.

- ◪ No revocation at all (unless in the child's best interest): Hawaii, Indiana, Louisiana (birth fathers only), Massachusetts, Nevada, New York (private adoption), North Dakota, Ohio, and Rhode Island.

- ◪ 3 days: Florida (if adoptive parents not identified), Illinois, Maine, and North Carolina (unborn infants and infants under 3 months of age).

- ◪ 4 days: Iowa

- 5 days after birth: Louisiana

- 7 days: North Carolina

- 10 days: Alaska, Arkansas, District of Columbia, Georgia, Minnesota, and Tennessee

- 11 days: Tennessee

- 14 days: Alabama

- 15 days: Oklahoma (out of court consents only), Virginia

- 20 days: Kentucky

- 21 days: Vermont

- 30 days: California (direct placement), and Maryland

- 45 days: New York (consent made outside of court)

- 60 days: Delaware

- any time before final decree: Connecticut, Idaho, Michigan, Missouri, Montana, Pennsylvania, South Dakota (final decree takes two years), and Washington

Court Process

The actual court procedure for an adoption is your final step in completing your adoption. When you get to this point, there should be some relief because you've gotten through the waiting and the process of meeting your child. Revocation of consent is the only real worry facing prospective adoptive parents at this point and this is an unlikely scenario.

Your adoption will be finalized in your state's family, juvenile, or surrogate's court. Your attorney will file your adoption petition and other paperwork and a date will be scheduled for the adoption. The court will review all the documents, including the home study and background checks. If the birth parent(s) is required to or chooses to give consent in front of the judge, this will happen in the courtroom. If the child is of the age set by the state, he will be asked to consent to the adoption. If a birth father could not be located and notice was given, the court will review the notice to make sure it meets the state's requirements. The adoption is then finalized and the judge signs the final order that makes it official and legal. It's important to remember that the actual court appearance is really just a formality. There's not going to be a trial and you're not going to questioned or cross-examined. The court is going to completely review the paperwork ahead of time and if there is a problem, your attorney will be notified. The actual court appearance is simply getting a bureaucratic stamp on your new family.

Judges spend most of their time dealing with cases where people are arguing or are unhappy, so it is a pleasant experience for them to handle an adoption where the result is a happy ending. Most judges will allow family and friends to join you in the courtroom if you like and you can bring your partner, even if he or she is not adopting with you at this time. Photos may be permitted. The court staff will often congratulate the adoptive parents and compliment the adoptive child. If the adoptive child is old enough to speak and understand what is happening, she is often made a part of the proceeding as well and is made to feel as if something very special has happened for her. Some judges will even give the child a certificate or a card to commemorate the special day.

Post Placement

With most agency adoptions, you will have some post-placement contact with the agency or with a social worker. You may have one or two post-placement visits from the social worker to make sure things are going smoothly and to offer some assistance with adjustments. These visits are usually nothing to worry about—no one is going to snatch your child out of your arms. The worker will prepare a post placement report which is filed with the agency (and may be filed with the court if required in your state).

Birth Certificates

After the adoption is finalized, you need to get an amended birth certificate for your adopted child. Your attorney will request this form. This new birth certificate will list the new parents (or parent if you are adopting alone), but maintain the child's birth date. This will be your child's official, legal birth certificate and there's no indication on it that an adoption took place—it looks similar to a regular birth certificate. The old birth certificate still exists as a state record, but it is not accessible. The adoption court proceeding also becomes sealed and inaccessible. This is why you hear about adult adoptees having difficulty finding their birth parents. The information about the birth becomes inaccessible to protect privacy.

Chapter 4

Second Parent Adoption

If you live in a state where you and your partner were not permitted to adopt simultaneously, or if you have a child of your own (adopted or biological) and want your partner to become the child's legal parent, you will need to do a second parent adoption, if it is permitted in your state.

Doing a second parent adoption is very important because if you don't, your partner has no legal ties to your child. He or she can't consent to medical care for the child, make decisions with schools, and if something should happen to you, your partner would have no legal standing to obtain guardianship or custody of your child. It is insulting to have to go through a separate legal process to ensure you have these rights, but for now doing so is the only way to ensure your child has two legal parents.

States Permitting Second Parent Adoptions

The following states permit same-sex second parent adoptions: California, Connecticut, Illinois, Massachusetts, New Jersey, New York, Pennsylvania, Vermont, and District of Columbia.

The following states have permitted some same-sex second parent adoptions, but have no clear rule: Alabama, Alaska, Delaware, Georgia, Hawaii, Indiana, Iowa, Louisiana, Maryland, Michigan, Minnesota, Nevada, New Hampshire, New Mexico, Ohio, Oregon, Rhode Island, Texas, and Washington.

If You Can't Do a Second Parent Adoption in Your State

If you live in a state that will not permit you to do a second parent adoption and you have a partner, you need to make some arrangements to protect your family. One of you will adopt the child and the other will not have any legal status in regard to the child. To protect your family, the legal parent will need to have a will drawn up listing the nonparent partner as guardian and giving specific reasons and details about their parent-child relationship. The legal parent will also need to execute written consents that authorize the nonlegal parent to make healthcare decisions for the child. Notify the school that the nonlegal parent has permission to pick the child up, talk to the school, access educational records, and make decisions for the child.

With all of that being said, there is nothing to stop you from acting as if both of you are the child's parents and holding yourselves out as such. Other people don't need to know the legalities of your situation and if you hold yourselves out as legal parents, you're likely to be accepted as such.

Deciding to Do a Second Parent Adoption

If you and your partner have made the decision to adopt together, a second parent adoption is just one more step in the red tape that you've got to get through. It is also just another part of the process if you use a fertility procedure (such as insemination or surrogacy) where only one partner is initially the legal parent. But if one of you had a child, and you became partnered with each other afterwards and want to do a second parent adoption, there are some things to consider.

First of all, you want to make sure that your commitment to each other is real. It might not be wise to do an adoption when you've only been together for six months or so, and many courts would question this as well. You obviously want to be sure you're in a long-term, committed relationship with your partner before you consider adoption. Taking on the responsibility for a child is something that shouldn't be done lightly or without serious consideration. It's also important to know that a second parent adoption can't just be undone should you break up or go your separate ways. It is a permanent legal change.

You also need to consider how your child feels. If your child is old enough to have an opinion, this might be something you'll want to discuss with her. And if you had your child while in another relationship, you need to get that other parent to consent to the adoption if he or she is a legal parent.

Notice or Consent

The parent that has custody of the child must consent to the adoption, and, in some states, must actually readopt the child as well (so that you are adopting the child together as a couple).

While this seems silly, it is simply a formality and does nothing to change the relationship between the child and the already existing parent.

If your child has another legal parent who is alive, that parent is entitled to some kind of notice of the adoption and the chance to refuse to consent. This other parent must consent to give up all rights to the child or fail to respond to the legal notice that is given in order for the adoption to be approved. Legal notice can be done by giving the parent papers explaining the plan about your partner adopting the child. In some states these documents can be mailed to the parent or personally served (given to him in person by a process server). If the other parent cannot be located, you may need to go through a process in which the notice is published in a newspaper.

Adoption is also possible when the other legal parent has his parental rights terminated by the court (such as in an abuse or neglect situation). In some states, if the other parent does not give consent, his rights can be terminated in certain circumstances, for example if he has not had any contact with the child for a long period of time. If your child has no other legal parent, you do not need to provide any kind of notice to anyone, but the adoption still must be approved by the court.

Preadoption Procedures

Some states waive the requirement for a home study in second parent adoptions (and some states have laws that require it, but permit judges to waive it when appropriate), but other states require the adopting partner (and the child's existing parent if she must also adopt the child) to go through the home study and background check process. Usually when a home study is required, the primary focus will be on the partner, her history, how long you have been together, and what kind of relationship your partner has with the child.

However, when it is required, the home study process is usually minimal—particularly if the first parent had to go through a home study to adopt the child originally. If a home study is required, try to use the same social worker you used for the first adoption (if this child was first adopted by one parent) because it will streamline things.

Home studies are not required for second parent adoptions in Alabama, Alaska, California, Connecticut, Georgia, Maryland, Michigan, Minnesota, Ohio, Pennsylvania, and Texas.

Home studies can be waived for adoptions in Nevada, New Hampshire, Oregon, and the District of Columbia.

Second Parent Adoption Process

Second parent adoptions are the type of adoption that can most easily be handled on your own without an attorney, although it is a good idea to hire an attorney to ensure that the case is handled properly (and if you are in a state that does not have a clear, solid track record about same sex adoptions, it would be wise to hire an experienced attorney). Some states do require representation by an attorney, no matter how simple your case.

> For up-to-the-minute information on same sex state adoption laws, go to *www.hrc.org*.

If you do choose to handle the adoption on your own, you need to contact the court in your state that handles adoptions to obtain forms and get information about the filing procedures. Remember that most second parent adoptions are routinely accepted in those states where they are permitted.

Following are sample second parent adoption forms for California that can be used as a reference in preparing for the adoption process.

Clerk stamps below when form is filed.

ADOPT-200 **Adoption Request**

If you are adopting more than one child, fill out an
adoption request for each child.

1 Your name(s) (adopting parent(s)):

a. _____

b. _____

Relationship to child: _____

Your address:

Street: _____

City: _____ State: _____ Zip: _____

Your phone #: (___) _____

Your lawyer (if you have one): (Name, address, phone #,
and State Bar #):

_____

_____

_____

> To keep other people from
> seeing what you entered on
> your form, please press the
> Clear This Form button at the
> end of the form when finished.

Court name and street address:

Superior Court of California, County of

Case Number:

2 Type of adoption: (Check one)

☐ Agency (name): _____
   ☐ Relative

☐ Independent

☐ International (name of agency): _____

☐ Stepparent/Domestic Partner

3 Information about the child:

a. The child's new name will be:

_____

b. ☐ Boy ☐ Girl

c. Date of birth: _____ Age: _____

d. Child's address (if different from yours):

Street: _____

e. Place of birth (if known):

City: _____

State: _____ Country: _____

f. If the child is 12 or older, does the child agree to
the adoption? ☐ Yes ☐ No

City: _____ State: _____ Zip: _____

4 Child's name before adoption (Fill out ONLY if this
is an independent, relative, or stepparent/domestic
partner adoption.): _____

5 Does the child have a legal guardian? ☐ Yes ☐ No

If yes, attach a copy of the Letters of Guardianship
and fill out below:

a. Date guardianship ordered: _____

b. County: _____

c. Case number: _____

(To be completed by the clerk of the superior court
if a hearing date is available.)

Hearing is set for:

Hearing Date Date: _____ Time: _____

Dept.: _____ Room: _____

Name and address of court if different from above:

_____

_____

To the person served with this request: If you do
not come to this hearing, the judge can order the
adoption without your input.

6 Is the child a dependent of the court? ☐ Yes ☐ No

If yes, fill out below:

Juvenile case number: _____

County: _____

Judicial Council of California, www.courtinfo.ca.gov
Rev. January 1, 2004, Mandatory Form
Family Code, §§ 8714, 8714.5, 8802, 8912, 9000; Welfare &
Institutions Code, § 16119; Cal. Rules of Court, rule 1464

Adoption Request

ADOPT-200, Page 1 of 3

American LegalNet, Inc.
www.USCourtForms.com →

Your name(s):_____

7 Child may have Indian ancestry: ☐ Yes ☐ No
If yes, attach Form ADOPT-220, Adoption of Indian Child

8 If this is an Agency Adoption:

a. I/We have received information about the Adoption Assistance Program, Regional Center, and mental health services available through Medi-Cal or other programs. ☐ Yes ☐ No

b. All persons with parental rights agree the child should be placed for adoption by the California Department of Social Services or a licensed adoption agency (Fam. Code, § 8700) and have signed a *Relinquishment* form approved by the California Department of Social Services except:

Name: _____ Relationship to child: _____

Name: _____ Relationship to child: _____

9 If this is an Independent Adoption:

a. A copy of the Adoptive Placement Agreement is attached. (Required in most independent adoptions; see Fam. Code, § 8802.)

b. I/We will file promptly with the department or delegated county adoption agency information required by the department in the investigation of the proposed adoption. ☐ Yes ☐ No

c. All persons with parental rights agree to the adoption and have signed the Adoptive Placement Agreement *Consent to Adoption* on a form approved by the California Department of Social Services except:

Name: _____ Relationship to child: _____

Name: _____ Relationship to child: _____

10 If this is a Stepparent/Domestic Partner Adoption:

a. The birth parent is ☐ in state ☐ out of state

(If out of state and unable to sign in the presence of the required official, the parent may sign his or her consent before a notary. (Fam. Code, § 9003 (b).))

b. Adopting parents married: _____ *(date)* OR Domestic partnership registered: _____ *(date)*.
(This does not affect the social worker's recommendation. Information is for court only. There is no waiting period.)

11 ☐ There is no presumed or biological father because the child was conceived by artificial insemination using semen provided to a medical doctor or a sperm bank. (Fam. Code, § 7613.)

12 Form ADOPT-310, *Contact After Adoption Agreement*:

☐ Is attached ☐ Will not be used ☐ Will be filed at least 30 days before the adoption hearing
☐ Undecided at this time

13 Name of birth parents if you know:

a. _____ *(mother)*

b. _____ *(father)*

14 ☐ The consent of the ☐ birth mother ☐ presumed father is not necessary because *(specify Fam. Code, § 8606 subdivision):* _____

Case Number:

Your name(s): _____

15 A court ended the parental rights of:

Name: _____ Relationship to child: _____

Name: _____ Relationship to child: _____

16 ☐ I/We will ask the court to end the parental rights of:

Name: _____ Relationship to child: _____

Name: _____ Relationship to child: _____

17 Each of the following persons with parental rights has not contacted his or her child in one year (Fam. Code, § 8604(b)):

Name: _____ Relationship to child: _____

Name: _____ Relationship to child: _____

18 Each of the following persons with parental rights has died:

Name: _____ Relationship to child: _____

Name: _____ Relationship to child: _____

19 Suitability for Adoption:
Each adopting parent:

a. Is at least 10 years older than the child   d. Has a suitable home for the child *and*

b. Will treat the child as his or her own   e. Agrees to adopt the child.

c. Will support and care for the child

20 I/We ask the court to approve the adoption and to declare that the adopting parent(s) and the child have the legal relationship of parent and child, with all the rights and duties of this relationship, including the right of inheritance.

21 If a lawyer is representing you in this case, he or she must sign here:

Date: _____ _____ ▶ _____

           Type or print your name   *Signature of Attorney for Adopting Parent*

22 I declare under penalty of perjury under the laws of the State of California that the information in this form is true and correct to my knowledge. This means if I lie on this form, I am guilty of a crime.

Date: _____ _____ ▶ _____

           Type or print your name   *Signature of Adopting Parent*

Date: _____ _____ ▶ _____

           Type or print your name   *Signature of Adopting Parent*

For your protection and privacy, please press the Clear This Form button after you have printed the form.

Print This Form	Clear This Form

| **ADOPT-210** **Adoption Agreement** | To keep other people from seeing what you entered on your form, please press the Clear This Form button at the end of the form when finished. |

(1) Your names *(adopting parents):*

a. _____

b. _____

Relationship to child: _____

Your address *(skip this if you have a lawyer):*

Street: _____

City: _____ State: _____ Zip: _____

Your phone number: (___) _____

Your lawyer *(if you have one): (Name, address, phone number, and State Bar number):* _____

_____

_____

_____

Fill in court name and street address:

Superior Court of California, County of

(2) Child's name:

Before adoption: _____

After adoption: _____

Date of birth: _____ Age: _____

Fill in case number:

Case Number:

(3) I am the child listed in **(2)** and I agree to the adoption.

Date: _____

_____
Type or print your name

▶
_____
Signature of Child (child must sign at hearing if 12 or older; optional if child is under 12)

(4) *If only one adopting parent, read and sign below:*

a. I am the adopting parent listed in **(1)**, and I agree that the child will:

(1) Be adopted and treated as my legal child (Fam. Code, § 8612(b)); *and*

(2) Have the same rights as a natural child of mine, including the right of inheritance.

Date: _____

_____
Type or print your name

▶
_____
Signature of Adopting Parent (sign at hearing)

b. I am the spouse or state-registered domestic partner of the adopting parent listed in **(1)**, and I agree to his or her adoption of the child.

Date: _____

_____
Type or print your name

▶
_____
Signature of Spouse or State-Registered Domestic Partner

Judicial Council of California, www.courtinfo.ca.gov
Revised January 1, 2009, Mandatory Form
Family Code, §§ 8602–8606, 8612, 9000;
Cal. Rules of Court, rule 1464

Adoption Agreement

ADOPT-210, Page 1 of 2
➡

American LegalNet, Inc.
www.USCourtForms.com

Case Number:

Your name: _____

(5) *If two adopting parents, read and sign below:*
We are the adopting parents listed in ①, and we agree that the child will:
(1) Be adopted and treated as our legal child (Fam. Code, § 8612(b));
(2) Have the same rights as a natural child of ours, including the right of inheritance;

and I agree to the other parent's adoption of the child.

Date: _____

► _____
Type or print your name   Signature of Adopting Parent (sign at hearing)

and I agree to the other parent's adoption of the child.

Date: _____

► _____
Type or print your name   Signature of Adopting Parent (sign at hearing)

(6) For *stepparent/domestic partner* adoptions only:
If you are the legal parent of the child listed in ②, *read and sign below:*
I am the legal parent of the child and the spouse or state-registered domestic partner of the adopting parent listed in ①, and I agree to his or her adoption of my child.

Date: _____

► _____
Type or print your name   Signature of Legal Parent (sign at hearing)

(7) **Executed:**

Date: _____

► _____
Judge (or Judicial Officer)

| Print This Form | For your protection and privacy, please press the Clear This Form button after you have printed the form. | Clear This Form |

ADOPT-215	Adoption Order

> To keep other people from seeing what you entered on your form, please press the Clear This Form button at the end of the form when finished.

(1) Your names *(adopting parents):*

a. _____

b. _____

Relationship to child: _____

Your address *(skip this if you have a lawyer):*

Street: _____

City: _____ State: _____ Zip: _____

Your phone number: (___) _____

Your lawyer *(if you have one): (Name, address, phone number, and State Bar number):* _____

_____

_____

_____

_____

Fill in court name and street address:

Superior Court of California, County of

(2) Child's name after adoption:

_____

Date of birth: _____ Age: _____

City: _____ State: _____ Country: _____

Fill in case number:

Case Number:

(3) Name of adoption agency: _____

(4) People present in court today *(date):* _____ in:

Dept.: _____ Div.: _____ Rm.: _____ Judge: _____

☐ Adopting parents ☐ Lawyer for adopting parents

☐ Child ☐ Child's lawyer

☐ Parent keeping parental rights *(stepparent/state-registered domestic partner name):* _____

☐ Other people present *(list name and relationship to child):*

a. _____

b. _____

If more, attach a sheet of paper, write "ADOPT-215, Item 4" at the top, and list additional names and relationships to child.

Judge will fill out section below.

(5) The judge finds that the child *(check all that apply):*

a. ☐ Is 12 or older and agrees to the adoption.

b. ☐ Is under 12.

(6) The judge has reviewed the report and other documents and evidence and finds that each adopting parent:

a. Is at least 10 years older than the child
d. Has a suitable home for the child *and*

b. Will treat the child as his or her own
e. Agrees to adopt the child.

c. Will support and care for the child

Judicial Council of California, www.courtinfo.ca.gov
Revised January 1, 2006, Mandatory Form
Family Code, §§ 8612, 8714, 8714.5, 8802, 8912, 9000

Adoption Order

ADOPT-215, Page 1 of 2

American LegalNet, Inc.
www.USCourtForms.com

	Case Number:

Your name: _____

(7) ☐ This case is a relative adoption petitioned under Family Code section 8714.5.
    ☐ The adopting relative   ☐ The child, who is 12 or older has requested that the child's name
    before adoption be listed on this order under section 8714.5(g).
    The child's name before adoption was: _____

(8) ☐ The child is an Indian child. The judge finds that this adoption meets the placement requirements of the
    Indian Child Welfare Act and that there is good cause to give preference to these adopting parents. The clerk will
    fill out (11) below.

(9) ☐ The judge approves the *Contact After Adoption Agreement* (ADOPT-310)
    ☐ As submitted   ☐ As amended on ADOPT-310

(10) The judge believes the adoption is in the child's best interest and orders this adoption.
The child's name after adoption will be: _____
The adopting parents and the child are now parent and child under the law, with all the rights and duties of the
parent-child relationship.

Date: _____   ▶ _____
                                    Judge (or Judicial Officer)

Clerk will fill out section below.

(11) **Clerk's Certificate of Mailing**
For the adoption of an Indian child, the Clerk certifies:
I am not a party to this adoption. I placed a filed copy of *(check all that apply)*:

☐ ADOPT-200, *Adoption Request*
☐ ADOPT-215, *Adoption Order*
☐ ADOPT-220, *Adoption of Indian Child*
☐ ADOPT-310, *Contact After Adoption Agreement*

in a sealed envelope, marked "Confidential," and addressed to:

    Chief, Division of Social Services
    Bureau of Indian Affairs
    1849 C Street, NW
    Mail Stop 310-SIB
    Washington, DC 20240

The envelope was mailed, with full postage, by U.S. mail from:

Place: _____ on *(date)*: _____

Date: _____   Clerk, by: _____ , Deputy

Print This Form	For your protection and privacy, please press the Clear This Form button after you have printed the form.	Clear This Form

Chapter 5

Domestic Agency Adoption

A domestic adoption agency is an agency in the United States that arranges adoptions of American-born children. A study published in *Adoption Quarterly* showed that 63 percent of public and private adoption agencies accept adoption applications from gay and lesbian singles or couples. The study also found that gays and lesbians were most often accepted by public agencies, Jewish affiliated agencies, and nonreligious agencies. Fundamentalist Christian and Catholic agencies were least likely to accept gays and lesbians. The study also revealed that most agencies that did accept gays do not actively reach out to gay communities. The agencies most likely to do so were public agencies. Of these, 50 percent of private agencies and 10 percent of public agencies that reported a willingness to accept adoption applications from gays also indicated that they would inform the birthparent of the adoptive parent's sexual orientation. Nearly a quarter of the private agencies allow the birth mother to make the selection of the adoptive parents.

Domestic agencies are not all alike and are divided into public and private agencies. A public agency is a state department of social services or department of family and children's services that places children for adoption who have been freed for adoption by state courts or who have been surrendered for adoption by their parents. These children are in foster care. Most of these children are not babies (foster care children can be any age, up to 18) and many are special needs children. There are many children available for adoption through these state agencies and there is less competition to adopt these children.

Private agencies are adoption agencies not run by the state. Some are nonprofit, while others are regular, for-profit businesses. Many are run by religious organizations while others are nonsectarian.

Public Agencies

Public agency adoptions have the same requirements as other types of adoptions, including the home study, background check, and court procedure to finalize the adoption. Public agency adoptions are usually the fastest and least expensive type of adoption. However, because the children tend to be older, the transition and adjustment period is often more difficult. There are several ways to adopt a child through a public agency.

All children that are available for adoption in a state are shown in the state's photo listings. The books show a photo of each child and offer a description of him or her.

> To view all state photo listings online, go to *http://photolisting.adoption.com/*.

Foster Care

The foster care system is a state run program that provides homes for children who have been removed from their homes because of abuse, neglect, and occasionally due to juvenile delinquency. Children who have been abandoned or voluntarily placed by parents with the state are also placed in foster care. Foster care is meant to be a temporary solution for a child while their parents deal with the court system, or the court determines that their parents abandoned them. Until a child is freed for adoption, the goal of foster care must be to reunite the family. Many times these children are returned to their parents, if the court decides that no abuse or neglect occurred or if the parents meet the requirements the court puts in place (such as counseling, childcare classes, maintaining a stable lifestyle, and so on) and the parents are deemed fit to care for the children.

Many times though, these children never return home. It's common procedure now in most states to move the case through the court system quickly so that the children are either returned home or are freed for adoption and do not languish in foster care for years. The federal Adoption and Safe Families Act states that if a child has been in foster care for at least 15 months or if his parents abandoned the child, parental rights can be terminated and the child freed for adoption. For the children that do not return home, the court severs the biological parents' legal ties to the children and frees them for adoption.

Many adoptions are done by the foster parents caring for the children, so becoming a foster parent is one route to public agency adoption. To become a foster parent you must first identify the private agencies that contract for foster care with the state (the state does not directly manage foster care programs and instead authorizes private agencies to train, select, and monitor foster parents). Prospective foster care parents must work with a public agency that handles the state agency's contract for foster care. See Chapter 8 for more information about becoming a foster parent.

Legal Risk Placement

Legal risk placement occurs when you accept a child into your home who you would like to adopt, but who has not yet been completely freed for adoption. The intent of this action is for the child to begin to develop a relationship with you and put down roots prior to the adoption. However, the child is not legally free for adoption yet, and something may happen that could prevent the adoption from occurring. While you are waiting for the child to be freed for adoption, you are acting as a foster care parent because the state still has custody and control of the child.

Traditional Adoption

Another method of adopting a child through a public agency is the traditional method where the child is not placed until the adoption is complete. The child remains in foster care until the legal process is finalized and then comes home to the adoptive parents. This is the least risky of all the public-agency adoption choices, but it can also be the most emotionally difficult for the child if she is old enough to understand what is happening. There is no transition period as there is in foster care placement or legal risk placement—suddenly your child moves into your home and you are the new parent.

This isn't a problem with very young children, but with older children it can be a complex emotional situation, and one that requires patience.

> You can find your state public adoption agency online at: *http://naic.acf.hhs.gov/general/nad/index.cfm.*

Public Agency Adoption Considerations

When adopting a child through a public agency, make sure to obtain full medical records and family histories if available. Before you agree to the adoption, you want to get as much information as you can. The child may have a history, characteristics, or background that does not work for you (it's important to be honest and face the fact that not every child is the right child for you), so you want to determine this as early in the process as possible. The caseworkers who manage the child while he is in foster care have access to the biological parents and can obtain this information. They can also provide information about assessments and evaluations that have been done while the child has been in foster care.

Because the child has biological parents that are usually alive and had some kind of relationship with them (no matter how dysfunctional), there are significant transition issues for the child and the adoptive parent. If the child is old enough, she will remember her biological parents and will have some kind of attachment to them (even if they were terrible parents). It takes a lot of time and patience to help children adjust. It also takes time for them to learn to trust adoptive parents. Many of these children were abused, mistreated, or emotionally damaged along with the process of being moved around to different foster homes. Moving into a loving, nurturing, permanent home can be a shock after all this upheaval.

Some adoptive parents report that their new children raid the refrigerator and gorge—certain that soon they would starve again. Other children have been known to steal from their new family members or harm new siblings. There are numerous behavioral issues that you might face after the adoption. A good counselor or therapist is essential to help everyone make a smooth adjustment.

Many public agency adoptive children have special needs. For this reason it is important to find out what evaluations have been done, what the specialists recommend, and what kind of care or treatment the child needs.

The National Resource Center for Special Needs Adoption can provide information and support for those adopting special needs children. You can contact them at: *http://www.nrcadoption.org/index.htm.*

Be sure to ask about the child's exposure to, or use of, drugs or alcohol and have a treatment plan in place to deal with these issues. Get detailed information about the child's behavior where he has lived and who has cared for him in the past. Ask for copies of all reports, evaluations, and assessments.

Another important issue is the child's biological relatives. While a court can sever legal ties between a child and her biological family, the court cannot change the emotional ties that exist. For this reason, some courts permit adoptive parents and biological relatives of the child to create and record kinship agreements. These agreements set out a plan for how the child will continue to have contact with important family members (such as grandparents, siblings, or aunts and uncles). This prevents a child from feeling totally cut off from her family and ethnic heritage. However, kinship agreements are not legally enforceable, so you don't need to worry that the adoption will be reversed if you are unable to honor them.

You may also want to consider a sibling group for adoption. Often an entire group of siblings is placed in foster care. Agencies are supposed to try to place them together so that they can maintain their relationship with each other. Taking in two or more children can be challenging, but it offers unique benefits because you can create a large family for yourself through one process, instead of adopting other children later. The children have a strong bond with each other and grow up with a biological relative in their family. There is also the satisfaction of knowing that you've taken in a group of children that are very difficult to find homes for.

Financial Assistance for Agency Adoptions

Because of the difficult nature of many public agency adoptions and because many of the children adopted do have special needs, there is special funding available to assist the parents in caring for the child after the adoption.

Title IV-E Assistance

Special needs children may qualify for federal funding assistance. The child may be receiving SSI (Social Security Insurance) payments already, but may also qualify for ASFA (Adoption and Safe Families Act) funding, which provides financial assistance for children who are adopted and:

- were receiving TANF (Temporary Assistance to Needy Families—in other words, welfare) in the birth home.
- were eligible for SSI in the birth home (they were disabled and were in a home that met certain financial requirements).

Adoption Assistance Agreement

An adoption assistance agreement is a contract between the adoptive parent or parents and the state agency, describing the ongoing monthly payments the state will make to the parents after the adoption is complete to help with the expense of raising the child. These are often a few hundred dollars per month.

> For information about state adoption subsidies, see *www.nacac.org/subsidy_stateprofiles.html.*

The agreement is made before the adoption takes place and is in effect as long as the child is a minor. The agreement may also include provisions providing assistance with the child's medical expenses (see Medicaid section that follows). Some states include additional funding amounts for children who are especially difficult to care for. These are known as LOC (Level of Care) payments.

The agreement is enforceable and if there is future disagreement about it, an administrative hearing is held to resolve the problem.

If you negotiate an agreement make sure it:

- ☑ is in writing.

- ☑ contains beginning and ending dates for the payments.

- ☑ specifies the amount of payments and any changes to the amount as the child ages.

- ☑ does not put excessive restrictions or requirements on you after the adoption occurs.

- ☑ specifies the reporting or certification you need to comply with to continue to receive payments.

- lists all services to be provided by the state.

- explains how subsidies or services can be increased or decreased and what kind of notice is required.

- describes Medicaid coverage for the child.

- explains what happens if you move out of state or if both adoptive parents die.

- describes what you need to do to get an administrative hearing should you need one.

- takes into account your child's needs and your family's situation.

Do not finalize your adoption until this document is signed.

Medicaid

A special needs child may qualify for Medicaid, and the state Medicaid program will pay many of her medical expenses both before and after the adoption. If you have a family healthcare policy, your child can also receive treatment under that plan, which may cover some of the things that Medicaid does not.

Private Agencies

Private agencies have infants as well as some older children to place for adoption, which is why some people prefer this route. An infant will take the longest to adopt (because you may need to wait for one to be born) while older children are placed more quickly. Most parents using private agencies are looking for babies.

Evaluating a Private Agency

The first step to working with a private agency is to select one carefully. Because you will pay an application fee, it is usually not a good idea to apply to more than one agency at a time. Your primary concern will be whether the agency is gay-friendly. You can call and ask or you can consult with other gay parents in your area.

> Some states provide special tuition assistance or waivers for foster care children who have been adopted. For more information, go to *http://www.nacac.org/ subsidyfactsheets/tuition.html.*

Once you've narrowed down your search to a few agencies, talk to the adoption specialist at your state department of social services. He can tell you what the agencies are like and what kind of information the state has available about them. Check with the Better Business Bureau in your state to determine if any complaints have been filed against the agency. Call the attorney general to ask if any complaints have been filed.

Fees and Expenses

Compare the home study costs and other fees that each agency charges. Less might not always be better if you feel a more expensive agency does a better job. Be absolutely certain that the agency and the social worker who does the home study are licensed in your state. Most states do not set limits on the fees an agency may charge, but hold them to the standard of what is "reasonable and customary."

Be skeptical if the agency takes money paid for the birth mother's expenses and places it in an escrow pool out of which it then pays all birth mother individual expenses for all birth mothers placing babies with the agency. With this method, you don't pay your birth mother's actual expenses, but instead pay an average cost that takes into account the high expenses some mothers have. Depending on the circumstance of your child's birth, this could be a good deal, or a bad deal. Most states require an accounting be made to the court, listing the expenses the adoptive parents have paid for.

Because most of the babies available for placement have not been born yet, there is the very real chance that the birth mother could change her mind before placement occurs or before the time period for legal consent ends. Ask what the agency's policy is about the fees should this happen—can you roll them over to use for another birth mother should the birth mother you choose change her mind? Are there some expenses that are not refundable (such as medical care during the pregnancy)?

Some states permit adoptive parents to pay for the birth mother's living expenses during her pregnancy (see later in this chapter). Adoptive parents pay for the medical expenses of both birth mother and baby, however the baby will not be covered by your health insurance plan until the child is placed with you, so these expenses are out of pocket expenses for you, unless the birth mother has health insurance coverage (or you purchase a policy for her).

Many adoptive parents feel a need to give the birth mother a gift after the birth. While this may seem like a wonderful gesture, it in fact can cause problems for you because many states prohibit any compensation to the birth mother for the adoption. This is intended to prevent the buying and selling of babies, but also prevents extravagant gifts. Small tokens of appreciation may be acceptable, but you need to check with your agency and your attorney before doing anything.

States that list certain expenses adoptive parents cannot pay or cap the payments for:

- Connecticut ($1,500 limit).

- Delaware (nothing other than court and legal expenses).

- Idaho ($2,000 limit).

- Illinois (does not allow lost wages, gifts, educational expenses).

- Indiana ($3,000 limit).

- Iowa (nothing other than room and board and counseling).

- Kentucky (does not allow for payment of birth parents' attorney fees).

- Maine (nothing other than legal costs, counseling, transportation to services, foster care, and living expenses).

- Minnesota (does not allow for lost wages, gifts, or educational expenses).

- Montana (does not allow for education, vehicle, salary, wages, or vacations or permanent housing for birth mother).

- New Hampshire (no gifts over $50 or educational expenses).

- New Mexico (nothing other than living expenses, medical costs, travel expenses, counseling and legal/court fees).

- Ohio (nothing other than medical costs, and legal expenses).

- Utah (nothing other than legal fees and expenses, medical care, maternity expenses, and living expenses).

◪ Wisconsin (does not permit lost wages or living expenses or anything other than counseling, maternity clothes, medical care, legal fees, birthing classes, and a $50 gift).

Chapter **7** provides information on the length of time living expenses can be paid.

Interstate Issues

In some states, there are not many children available for adoption within the state. If this is the case for you, you may want to consider adopting a child from another state. To do so though, you and the agency must be in compliance with the Interstate Compact, a federal law that governs how children are transported between states for adoption purposes. Each state has an Interstate Compact administrator, and the administrators in the state you live in and the state you are adopting from must both agree to the adoption. Your adoption agency and attorney will handle this technicality for you. It is an added complication, but it is by no means as complicated as adopting from another country.

Ethnic Concerns

A federal law, called the Multiethnic Placement Act, denies federal funding to adoption agencies that delay or deny placement because of race (in other words, wait to place a child only with parents of the same race as that child). If you are interested in adopting a child with an ethnic background that is different than yours, ask if the agency you are using or considering complies with this statute. If you believe you've been turned down for an adoption because of race, talk to your adoption attorney or contact your state attorney general.

Chapter 6

International Adoption

International adoption is the adoption of a child from a country outside the United States. It is an excellent choice if you want to adopt a young child, but don't want to wait to find a birth mother or new baby and don't mind adopting a child who is not a newborn. The procedure is not as complicated as you might expect it to be and the costs end up being about the same as a domestic adoption (when you factor in travel costs). The procedure is similar to those for domestic adoptions, but involves extra steps, such as dealing with the Bureau of Homeland Security's BCIS (Bureau of Citizenship and Immigration Services—once known as the Immigration and Naturalization Service—INS) as well as overseas courts.

Unfortunately, most countries will not allow adoption by openly gay people, so in order to accomplish an international adoption, you will need to keep that information to yourself. As in domestic adoptions, if you are directly asked, you should not lie, but if you do not mention it, you have not done anything wrong. A study in *Adoption Quarterly* found that even though most countries have a policy against allowing adoption by gay parents, 65.5 percent of U.S. adoption agencies that handle international adoptions are willing to accept applications from lesbians and gays. At these agencies, they report that the caseworkers do not ask questions about sexual orientation.

If you have a partner and choose to do an international adoption, you will need to do it in two parts, with one parent adopting the child first and the second parent doing a second parent adoption, if permitted in your state.

Choosing an Agency

You will most likely need to work with an agency to do an international adoption, because children are, for the most part, available mainly through agencies in the foreign countries. Some private U.S. agencies handle only domestic adoption or only international adoption, while others handle both types, so you'll need to do a little research to find some agencies to consider. When interviewing international agencies, ask these questions:

- What countries do you have agreements with?

- How many children have you placed from each of these countries in the last year?

- How long have you worked with each country?

- Do the overseas agencies you work with also work with other U.S. agencies?

- ▰ Who works overseas for your agency?

- ▰ How do babies come into the programs?

- ▰ How long will the process take?

- ▰ If parents must travel to complete the adoption, what arrangements and assistance do you provide for the trip? Is a travel agency involved?

- ▰ Is an escort provided?

- ▰ Can the agency be reached by phone outside of business hours while you are overseas?

- ▰ What access is provided to the children overseas?

- ▰ Can the agency provide referrals to Western doctors in the overseas country while we are there should the need arise?

- ▰ Are you licensed in this state?

- ▰ How long have you been doing international adoptions?

- ▰ If a parent turns down a child, can she adopt another child?

- ▰ What kinds of services do you provide after placement?

Read the list of agencies accredited by the Joint Council of International Children's Services at *www.jcics.org*, or at the International Adoption Consortium at *www.welcomegarden.com/resources_by_state.html*.

For more information on choosing an international adoption agency, see: *http://www.adopting.org/choosagn.html*.

Choosing a Country

At the time this book was written, international adoptions were mainly available from the following countries:

- ▨ Bolivia

- ▨ Bulgaria

- ▨ Cambodia

- ▨ China

- ▨ Columbia

- ▨ Guatemala

- ▨ Haiti

- ▨ India

- ▨ Mexico

- ▨ Philippines

- ▨ Romania

- ▨ Russia and former Soviet republics

- ▨ South Korea (note that to date, this is the only country you do not need to actually travel to in order to adopt a child; the child flies to the United States with a chaperone)

- ▨ Thailand

- ▨ Vietnam

Each country has its own requirements. For example, Russia requires that parents make two trips to the country— one to identify the child and the second to adopt him. You should learn about the requirements in the countries you are considering before making a final choice.

Some parents go into the adoption process knowing which country they want to adopt from, while others have no prefer- ence and choose a country that seems to fit them best once they have done some research. You may have ties to a certain country and feel more comfortable adopting a child from there, or you might choose a country based on its requirements and procedures. There is no wrong way to make the choice.

> The U.S. Department of State has country specific information available at *www.travel.state.gov* in the adoption section. The document for each country on this site spells out that country's requirements and also lists U.S. agencies that handle adoptions from that country.

Choosing a Child

In some countries, you go to the orphanage and actually select a child that appeals to you, while other countries assign a child to you. If you adopt from South Korea, you will never meet your child until she is delivered to you at the airport here in the United States, although you will see photos.

Healthcare standards in the countries children are adopted from are of particular concern to many adoptive parents. Because the standard of healthcare and prenatal care varies greatly overseas, many children available for placement are developmentally delayed or suffering from a health problem. Before you finalize your choice (and get emotionally attached to a child), obtain photos or video tape as well as whatever medical records can be translated into English, and have them reviewed by a pediatrician who specializes in evaluating children for overseas adoptions. You can then make an informed choice and decide if this child is one you will be able to care for. Realize that some parents have different abilities than others and you should only select a child whom you feel you can provide good care for and feel comfortable with.

If you will not have access to the child's medical documents before you travel overseas, make arrangements before you leave to fax or express ship these to the doctor while you are there. He can evaluate the child from the records and make an educated inference about what kinds of problems the child may be experiencing. Note that it is more difficult to reject a child once you have traveled to the country and met her.

The American Academy of Pediatrics provides a list of pediatricians specializing in adoption at: *www.aap.org/sections/adoption/adopt-states/adoption-map.html.*

Your child must be released for adoption by his country of origin. Only children who are completely released for adoption will be eligible for adoption in the eyes of the U.S. government. You will need your agency's help to obtain this release.

Dealing With Paperwork

Your application for the adoption will be made to your local agency. They will be your primary contact throughout the entire adoption process and will handle most of the contacts with the overseas agency and officials there. The application and home study process for an international adoption is similar to that required for a domestic adoption. All of these documents must be translated and then approved by the agency in the country you are adopting from, so this is an extra step (your agency will arrange for the translation). Additionally, many of the documents you provide must be authenticated, meaning they must bear a raised seal from the agency or office issuing them (there is an additional fee for obtaining authenticated copies). You may need to include photos of your home for review by the overseas agency.

In addition to the usual home study and application, you will also need to obtain preliminary BCIS approval. You are not eligible if you have been convicted of a felony or certain misdemeanors.

The International Adoption Process

Because each country has its own requirements, there is no one set procedure for international adoptions. The procedure you must follow in the United States. is the same however.

You will need to complete the application, home study process (your home study will be used both by the agency as well as the BCIS to determine that you are qualified to adopt), and background check (which is also submitted to BCIS). Fingerprints must be completed on form FD-258 and will be done at the BCIS office using a form they provide. Fingerprinting will occur at your home BCIS office if you are in the United States or at the embassy or consulate if you are abroad.

Before you even have a child selected for adoption, you can begin the adoption process by filing form I-600A, Orphan Petition, which begins the process of classifying the child you will adopt as an immediate relative. The fee for filing is $460. All BCIS forms must be filed at your local office. You also need to file form I-864, which is an affidavit about your ability to support a child.

> Find the necessary forms online at *http://uscis.gov/*
> *graphics/formsfee/forms*.

Once you have been approved to adopt by the agency and the U.S. government, you will need to learn about the requirements for finalizing the adoption in the country your child is from. This may include a court appearance in that country's court. If so, it is important that you have a translator along (your agency can help you arrange for this). You may need to travel to the country and stay there for a period of time before you are permitted to adopt. You may need to appear in court in the country or at a government office to finalize the adoption. Obtain several official copies of any documents you are provided by the officials you work with in the country.

One thing that is important to understand is that government and official processes can be very different in other countries. There may be unexpected delays, situations in which money must change hands to speed things along, as well as irregular hours and unexpected requests for additional documentation. If you know this going in, it won't be so frustrating. Because of these complications, it is very important to work with an agency that has worked in this country before and which completely understands the procedures and problems. You also must be sure you will have a translator or guide when you are there who is familiar with the process and knows how to get things done. For a good idea of what to expect, read Kevin McGarry's book, *Fatherhood for Gay Men*, which is a personal account of his adoptions.

Dealing With Immigration

To bring your child to the United States, you must do the following:

- ▨ Use form I-600 to petition to have the identified child classified as an immediate relative (if you filed for I-600A there is no fee for form I-600. If you did not, there is a $460 fee).

◪ Apply for the child to immigrate to the United States.

You must physically see your child in person before you are permitted to adopt him. If you are not adopting your child in the country of origin and instead are only adopting her in the United States, be sure you check the box on the Orphan Petition indicating this.

Citizenship

Part of the adoption process is helping your child become an American citizen. There are several ways this can occur.

Child Citizenship Act of 2000

This federal law allows an internationally adopted child to automatically become an U.S. citizen. In order for the act to apply the child must:

◪ have one American parent (adoptive)

◪ be legally adopted by this parent

◪ be under age 18

◪ live with the American parent who has custody of the child

◪ be admitted to the United Sates as an immigrant for lawful permanent residence (under an IR4 visa)

If these requirements are satisfied, your child will automatically be granted citizenship when the adoption is legal in the United States.

To become a citizen, your child's passport (from her country of origin) will be stamped with BCIS Stamp I-551. You can then apply for a passport for your child (a passport will be your child's proof of citizenship). To apply for a passport, you need the following:

- DSP-11, application for a passport

- two (2) identical photographs (2 X 2 inches in size)

- parent's valid identification

- certified adoption decree (with English translation, if necessary)

- the child's foreign passport with BCIS Stamp I-551 or the child's resident alien card

- the fee payment

Visas

A visa is a document that gives tentative permission for the child to enter the United States from a foreign country. The visa itself is not complete authority because immigration officials at the point of entry have the final say upon the child's entrance to the country.

To apply for a visa for your child, use form IR-3 (for children adopted in a foreign country) or IR-4 for children that will be adopted in the United States. The application must be submitted to the U.S. embassy or consular office in the country the child is being adopted from. The child must be seen by the consular or embassy official and must also be examined by a physician approved by the embassy/consulate. Certain contagious diseases may be the basis for temporarily denying a visa. The adoptive parent must appear at the consulate or embassy for an interview. There is a $260 fee to apply for the visa, and a $65 fee for the issuance of the visa.

Readoption

Because U.S. courts are not required to legally recognize an adoption completed in a foreign country, it is a good idea to adopt your child in your state court, even if you have already completed an adoption process in the child's country of origin.

Changes in Adoption Law

At the time this book was published, the United States was close to approving changes to international adoption law. The Hague Convention on Intercountry Adoption is an international document that provides procedures and rules for how international adoptions are handled and processed. If the United States does adopt these rules, there will be some changes to the way international adoptions are handled to ensure that the children placed for adoption are truly available. Some say the changes will complicate the international adoption process, while others say the changes provide important protections for all involved in the process. To read more about this, see *http://uscis.gov/graphics/services/HagueFS.pdf*. For more information on international adoption, see *How to Adopt Internationally: A Guide for Agency-Directed and Independent Adoptions* by Jean Nelson Erichsen and Heino R. Erichsen.

Forms Checklist for International Adoption

- birth certificates (yours and your child's)

- child abuse clearance

- divorce/death certificate if you were married in a heterosexual marriage

- financial statement

- foreign adoption/custody decree

- foreign birth certificate for the child

- foreign passport for the child

- home study

- letters of recommendation

- "orphan" status document

- photographs of the family

- photographs of the child

- physician's report about you

- physician's report of the child

- police certificate

- power of attorney

- verification of employment

- 1040 (front two pages)

- passports (if you will be traveling to get your child)

- Form I-600A and/or I-600 Orphan Petition

- Form I-864 Affidavit of Support

- Form IR-3 or IR-4 to apply for a visa

Following are sample forms I-600A, I-600, and 213A which are all relevant to the adoption process.

OMB No. 1615-0028; Expires 08/31/08

Department of Homeland Security
U.S. Citizenship and Immigration Services

**I-600A, Application for Advance
Processing of Orphan Petition**

Instructions

What Is the Purpose of This Form?

This form is used by a U.S. citizen who plans to adopt a foreign-born orphan but does not have a specific child in mind. "Advance Processing" enables USCIS to first adjudicate the application that relates to the qualifications of the applicant(s) as a prospective adoptive parent(s).

Additionally, this form may be used in cases where the child is known and the prospective adoptive parent(s) are traveling to the country where the child is located. However, it is important that prospective adoptive parent(s) be aware that the child must remain in the foreign country where he or she is located until the processing is completed.

NOTE: This Form I-600A application is not a petition to classify an orphan as an immediate relative. Form I-600, Petition to Classify Orphan as an Immediate Relative, is used for that purpose.

1. What Are the Eligibility Requirements?

A. Eligibility for advance processing application (Form I-600A).

An application for advance processing may be filed by a married U.S. citizen and spouse. The spouse of the applicant does not need to be a U.S. citizen; however, he or she must be in a lawful immigration status. An application for advance processing may also be filed by an unmarried U.S citizen who is at least 24 years of age, provided that he or she will be at least 25 at the time of adoption and the filing of an orphan petition on behalf of a child.

B. Eligibility for orphan petition (Form I-600).

In addition to the requirements concerning the citizenship and age of the applicant described above in Instruction **1. A.** when a child is located and identified the following eligibility requirements will apply:

(1) Child.

Under U.S. immigration law, an orphan is an alien child who has no parents because of the death or disappearance of, abandonment or desertion by, or separation or loss from both parents.

An orphan is also a child who has only one parent who is not capable of taking care of the orphan and who has, in writing, irrevocably released the orphan for emigration and adoption.

A petition to classify an alien as an orphan (Form I-600) may not be filed on behalf of a child who is present in the United States, unless that child is in parole status and has not been adopted in the United States.

The petition must be filed before the child's 16th birthday.

(2) Adoption abroad.

If the orphan was adopted abroad, it must be established that both the married applicant and spouse or the unmarried applicant personally saw and observed the child prior to or during the adoption proceedings. The adoption decree must show that a married prospective adoptive parent and spouse adopted the child jointly or that an unmarried prospective parent was at least 25 years of age at the time of the adoption and filing of Form I-600.

(3) Proxy adoption abroad.

If both the applicant and spouse or the unmarried applicant did not personally see and observe the child prior to or during the adoption proceedings abroad, the applicant (and spouse, if married) must submit a statement indicating the applicant's (and, if married, the spouse's) willingness and intent to readopt the child in the United States. If requested, the applicant must submit a statement by an official of the state in which the child will reside that readoption is permissible in that State. In addition, evidence must be submitted to show compliance with the preadoption requirements, if any, of that State.

(4) Preadoption requirements.

If the orphan has not been adopted abroad, the applicant and spouse or the unmarried applicant must establish that the child will be adopted in the United States by the prospective applicant and spouse jointly or by the unmarried prospective applicant, and that the preadoption requirements, if any, of the State of the orphan's proposed residence have been met.

2. What Are the Requirements to File?

A. Proof of U. S. citizenship of the prospective adoptive parent(s).

(1) If a U.S. citizen by birth in the United States, submit a copy of the birth certificate issued by the civil registrar, vital statistics office or other civil authority. If a birth certificate is not available, submit a statement from the appropriate civil authority certifying that a birth certificate is not available. In such a situation, secondary evidence must be submitted, including:

- **Church records** bearing the seal of the church showing the baptism, dedication or comparable rite occurred within two months after birth and showing the date and place of the prospective adoptive parent's birth, date of the religious ceremony and the names of the parents;

- School Records issued by the authority (perferably the first school attended) showing the date of admission to the school, prospective adoptive parent's date of birth or age at the time, the place of birth and the names of the parents;

- **Census records** (state or federal) showing the name, place of birth, date of birth or age of the prospective adoptive parent listed;

- **Affidavits** sworn to or affirmed by two persons who were living at the time and who have personal knowledge of the date and place of birth in the United States of the prospective adoptive parent. Each affidavit should contain the following information regarding the person making the affidavit: his or her full name, address, date and place of birth and relationship to the prospective adoptive parent, if any, and full information concerning the event and complete details of how the affiant acquired knowledge of the birth; or

- An unexpired **U.S. passport**, initially issued for ten years, may also be submitted as proof of U.S. citizenship.

(2) If the prospective adoptive parent was born outside the United States, submit a copy of one of the following:

- Certificate of Naturalization or Certificate of Citizenship issued the by U.S. Citizenship and Immigration Services (USCIS) or the former Immigration and Naturalization Service (INS);

- Form FS-240, Report of Birth Abroad of a Citizen of the United States, issued by an American embassy;

- An unexpired U.S. passport initally issued for ten years; or

- An original statement from a U.S. consular officer verifying the applicant's U.S. citizenship with a valid passport.

  NOTE: Proof of the lawful immigration status of the applicant's spouse, if applicable, must be submitted. If the spouse is not a U.S. citizen, proof of her or his lawful immigration status, such as Form I-551, Permanent Resident Card; Form I-94, Arrival-Departure Record; or a copy of the biographic pages of the spouse's passport and the nonimmigrant visa pages showing an admission stamp may be submitted.

B. Proof of marriage of applicant and spouse.

The married applicant must submit a copy of the certificate of marriage and proof of termination of all prior marriages of himself or herself and spouse. In the case of an unmarried applicant who was previously married, submit proof of termination of all prior marriages.

NOTE: If any change occurs in the applicant('s) marital status while the application is pending, immediately notify the USCIS office where the application was filed.

C. Home Study.

The home study must include a statement or attachment recommending or approving the adoption or proposed adoption, and be signed by an official of the responsible State agency in the State of the proposed residence or of an agency authorized by that State.

In the case of a child adopted abroad, the statement or attachment must be signed by an official of an appropriate public or private adoption agency which is licensed in the U.S.

The home study must be prepared by an entity (individual or organization) licensed or otherwise authorized under the laws of the State of the orphan's proposed residence to conduct research and preparation for a home study, including the required personal interviews.

If the recommending agency is licensed, the recommendation must specify that it is licensed, the State in which it is licensed, its license number, if any, and the period of validity of the license.

However, the research, including the interview and the preparation of the home study may be done by an individual or group in the United States or abroad that is satisfactory to the recommending entity.

A responsible State agency or licensed agency may accept a home study made by an unlicensed or foreign agency and use that home study as a basis for a favorable recommendation.

The home study must provide an assessment of the capabilities of the prospective adoptive parent(s) to properly parent the orphan and must include a discussion of the following areas:

(1) An assessment of the financial ability of the adoptive or prospective adoptive parents or parent.

(2) A detailed description of the living accommodations where the adoptive or prospective adoptive parents or parent currently reside(s).

(3) If the prospective adoptive parent or parents are residing abroad at the time of the home study, a description of the living accommmodations where the child will reside in the United States, with the prospective adoptive parent or parents, if known.

(4) An assessment of the physical, mental and emotional capabilities of the adoptive or prospective adoptive parent or parents in relation to rearing and educating the child.

(5) An explanation regarding any history of abuse or violence or any complaints, charges, arrests, citations, convictions, prison terms, pardons, rehabilitation decrees for breaking or violating any law or ordinance by the prospective adoptive parent(s) or any additional adult member of the household over age 18 years.

  NOTE: Having committed any crime of moral turpitude or a drug-related offense does not necessarily mean that the prospective adoptive parent(s) will be found not qualified to adopt an orphan. However, failure to disclose such information may result in denial of this application and/or any subsequent petition for an orphan.

D. Biometric services.

As part of the USCIS biometric services requirement, the following persons must be fingerprinted in connection with this application:

- The married prospective adoptive parent and spouse, if applicable, and

- Each additional adult member 18 years of age or older, of the prospective adoptive parent(s)' household. **NOTE:** Submit a copy of the birth certificate of each qualifying household member over 18.

If necessary, USCIS may also take each person's photograph and signature as part of the biometric services.

(1) **Petitioners residing in the United States.** After filing this petition, USCIS will notify each person in writing of the time and location where they must go to be fingerprinted. Failure to appear to be fingerprinted or for other biometric services may result in denial of this application.

(2) **Petitioners residing abroad.** Completed fingerprint cards (Forms FD-258) must be submitted with this application. Do not bend, fold or crease the completed fingerprint cards. The fingerprint cards must be prepared by a U.S. embassy or consulate, USCIS office or U.S. military installation.

3. General Filing Instructions.

A. Type or print legibly in black ink.

B. If extra space is needed to complete any item, attach a continuation sheet, indicate the item number, and date and sign each sheet.

C. Translations.

Any foreign language document must be accompanied by a full English translation that the translator has certified as complete and correct. The translator must also certify that he or she is competent to translate the foreign language into English.

D. Copies.

If these instructions tell you to submit a copy of a particular document, you do not have to send the original document. However, if there are stamps, remarks, notations, etc., on the back of the original documents, also submit copies of the back of each document(s). You will not have to submit the original document unless USCIS requests it.

There are times when USCIS must request an original copy of a document. In that case, the original document is generally returned after it has been reviewed.

E. Certification.

The "Certification of Prospective Adoptive Parent" block of Form I-600A must be executed by the prospective adoptive parent. The spouse, if applicable, must execute the **"Certification of Married Prospective Adoptive Parent Spouse"** block on **Page 2** of the form. Failure to do so will result in the rejection of the Form I-600A.

F. Submission of the Application.

A prospective adoptive parent residing in the United States should send the completed application to the USCIS office having jurisdiction over his or her place of residence. A prospective adoptive parent residing outside the United States should consult the nearest American consulate for the overseas or stateside USCIS office designated to act on the application.

4. What Is the Fee.

A fee of **$545.00** must be submitted for filing this application.

In addition to the fee for the application, there is a **$70.00** biometric services fee for fingerprinting every adult person living in the household in the United States where the child will reside.

For example, if an application is filed by a married couple residing in the United States with one additional adult member in their household, the total fees that must be submitted would be **$755.00 ($545.00** for the petition and **$210.00** for the biometric services fees for fingerprinting the three adults).

NOTE: If the prospective adoptive parent(s) and any other adult members of the household are residing abroad at the time of filing, they are exempt from paying the biometric services fee for fingerprinting. However, they may have to pay fingerprinting fees charged by the U.S. Department of State or military installation.

The fee will not be refunded, whether the application is approved or not. Do not mail cash. All checks or money orders, whether U.S. or foreign, must be payable in U.S. currency at a financial institution in the United States. When a check is drawn on the account of a person other than yourself, write your name on the face of the check. If the check is not honored, USCIS will charge you $30.00.

Pay by check or money order in the exact amount. Make the check or money order payable to the **Department of Homeland Security**, unless:

A. You live in Guam, make the check or money order payable to the "Treasurer, Guam" or

B. You live in the U.S. Virgin Islands, make your check or money order payable to the "Commissioner of Finance of the Virgin Islands."

How to Check If the Fee Is Correct.

The fee on this form is current as of the edition date appearing in the lower right corner of this page. However, because USCIS fees change periodically, you can verify if the fee is correct by following one of the steps below:

- Visit our website at **www.uscis.gov** and scroll down to "Forms and E-Filing" to check the appropriate fee, or

- Review the Fee Schedule included in your form package, if you called us to request the form, or

- Telephone our National Customer Service Center at **1-800-375-5283** and ask for the fee information.

NOTE: If your petition or application requires a biometric services fee for USCIS to take your fingerprints, photograph or signature, you can use the same procedure above to confirm the biometrics fee.

5. What Should You Do After Locating and/or Identifying a Child or Children?

Form I-600, Petition to Classify Orphan as an Immediate Relative, is filed when a child has been located and/or identified for the prospective adoptive parent(s). A new fee is not required if Form I-600 is filed within 18 months from the approval date of the Form I-600A application. If approved in the home study for more than one orphan, the prospective adoptive parent(s) may file a petition for each of the additional children to the maximum number approved. If the orphans are siblings, no additional filing fee is required. However, if the orphans are not siblings, an additional filing fee is required for each orphan beyond the first orphan.

NOTE: Approval of an advance processing application does not guarantee that the orphan petition(s) will be approved.

Form I-600 must be accompanied by all the evidence required by the instructions of that form, except where provided previously with Form I-600A.

Generally, Form I-600 should be submitted at the USCIS office where the advance processing application, Form I-600A, was filed. Prospective adoptive parent(s) going abroad to adopt or locate a child may file Form I-600 with either the USCIS office or American consulate or embassy having jurisdiction over the place where the child is residing or will be located, unless the case is being retained at the USCIS office stateside.

USCIS has offices in the following countries: Austria, China, Cuba, the Dominican Republic, El Salvador, Germany, Ghana, Great Britain, Greece, Guatemala, Haiti, Honduras, India, Italy, Jamaica, Kenya, Korea, Mexico, Pakistan, Panama, Peru, the Philippines, Russia, South Africa, Thailand and Vietnam.

6. Penalties.

Willful false statements on this form or supporting documents may be punished by fine or imprisonment. U.S. Code, Title 18, Sec. 1001 (Formerly Sec. 80.)

7. Authority for Collecting Information.

8 U.S.C 1154 (a). Routine uses for disclosure under the Privacy Act of 1974 have been published in the Federal Register and are available upon request. USCIS will use the information to determine immigrant eligibility. Submission of the information is voluntary, but failure to provide any or all of the information may result in denial of the application.

8. USCIS Forms and Information.

To order USCIS forms, call our toll-free number at **1-800-870-3676**. You can also get USCIS forms and information on laws, regulations and procedures by telephoning our **National Customer Service Center** at **1-800-375-5283** or visiting our internet website at **www.uscis.gov.**

9. Use InfoPass for Appointments.

As an alternative to waiting in line for assistance at your local USCIS office, you can now schedule an appointment through our internet-based system, **InfoPass**. To access the system, visit our website at **www.uscis.gov**. Use the **InfoPass** appointment scheduler and follow the screen prompts to set up your appointment. **InfoPass** generates an electronic appointment notice that appears on the screen. Print the notice and take it with you to your appointment. The notice gives the time and date of your appointment, along with the address of the USCIS office.

10. Reporting Burden.

A person is not required to respond to a collection of information unless it displays a currently valid OMB control number. Public reporting burden for this collection of information is estimated to average 30 minutes per response, including the time for reviewing instructions, searching existing data sources, gathering and maintaining the data needed, and completing and reviewing the collection of information. Send comments regarding this burden estimate or any other aspect of this collection of information, including suggestions for reducing this burden, to U.S. Citizenship and Immigration Services, Regulatory Management Division, 111 Massachusetts Avenue, N.W., Washington, DC 20529; OMB No. 1615-0028. **Do not mail your completed application to this address.**

OMB No. 1615-0028; Expires 08/31/08

Department of Homeland Security
U.S. Citizenship and Immigration Services

**I-600A, Application for Advance
Processing of Orphan Petition**

Do not write in this block.   **For USCIS Use Only.**

It has been determined that the:
☐ Married   ☐ Unmarried

prospective adoptive parent will furnish proper care to a beneficiary orphan if admitted to the United States.
There:
☐ are   ☐ are not

preadoptive requirements in the State of the child's proposed residence.

The following is a description of the preadoption requirements, if any, of the State of the child's proposed residence:

_____

The preadoption requirements, if any,:
☐ have been met.   ☐ have not been met.

Fee Stamp

DATE OF FAVORABLE DETERMINATION

DD

DISTRICT

File number of applicant, if applicable.

Please type or print legibly in black ink.

This application is made by the named prospective adoptive parent for advance processing of an orphan petition.

BLOCK I - Information about the prospective adoptive parent.

1. My name is: (Last) (First) (Middle)

2. Other names used (including maiden name if appropriate):

3. I reside in the U.S. at: (C/O if appropriate) (Apt. No.)

(Number and Street) (Town or City) (State) (Zip Code)

4. Address abroad (If any): (Number and Street) (Apt. No.)

(Town or City) (Province) (Country)

5. I was born on: *(mm/dd/yyyy)*

In: (Town or City) (State or Province) (Country)

6. My telephone number is: (Include Area Code)

7. My marital status is:
☐ Married
☐ Widowed
☐ Divorced
☐ Single
  ☐ I have never been married.
  ☐ I have been previously married _____ time(s).

8. If you are now married, give the following information:

Date and place of present marriage *(mm/dd/yyyy)*

Name of present spouse (include maiden name of wife)

Date of birth of spouse *(mm/dd/yyyy)* Place of birth of spouse

Number of prior marriages of spouse

My spouse resides ☐ With me ☐ Apart from me (provide address below)

(Apt. No.) (No. and Street) (City) (State) (Country)

9. I am a citizen of the United States through:
☐ Birth ☐ Parents ☐ Naturalization

If acquired through naturalization, give name under which naturalized, number of naturalization certificate, and date and place of naturalization.

If not, submit evidence of citizenship. See Instruction 2.a(2).

If acquired through parentage, have you obtained a certificate in your own name based on that acquisition?
☐ No ☐ Yes

Have you or any person through whom you claimed citizenship ever lost United States citizenship?
☐ No ☐ Yes (If Yes, attach detailed explanation.)

Received	Trans. In	Ret'd Trans. Out	Completed

BLOCK II - General information.

10. Name and address of organization or individual assisting you in locating or identifying an orphan

(Name)

_____

(Address)

11. Do you plan to travel abroad to locate or adopt a child?

☐ Yes   ☐ No

12. Does your spouse, if any, plan to travel abroad to locate or adopt a child?

☐ Yes   ☐ No

13. If the answer to Question 11 or 12 is "Yes," give the following information:

    a. Your date of intended departure _____

    b. Your spouse's date of intended departure _____

    c. City, province _____

14. Will the child come to the United States for adoption after compliance with the preadoption requirements, if any, of the State of proposed residence?

☐ Yes   ☐ No

15. If the answer to Question 14 is "No," will the child be adopted abroad after having been personally seen and observed by you and your spouse, if married?

☐ Yes   ☐ No

16. Where do you wish to file your orphan petition?

The USCIS office located at

_____

The American Embassy or Consulate at

_____

17. Do you plan to adopt more than one child?

☐ Yes   ☐ No

If "Yes," how many children do you plan to adopt?

Certification of prospective adoptive parent.

I certify, under penalty of perjury under the laws of the United States of America, that the foregoing is true and correct and that I will care for an orphan/orphans properly if admitted to the United States.

_____
(Signature of Prospective Adoptive Parent)

_____
Executed on (Date)

Certification of married prospective adoptive parent spouse.

I certify, under penalty of perjury under the laws of the United States of America, that the foregoing is true and correct and that my spouse and I will care for an orphan/orphans properly if admitted to the United States.

_____
(Signature of Prospective Adoptive Parent Spouse)

_____
Executed on (Date)

Signature of person preparing form, if other than petitioner.

I declare that this document was prepared by me at the request of the petitioner and is based entirely on information of which I have knowledge.

_____
(Signature)

_____
Street Address and Room or Suite No./City/State/Zip Code

_____
Executed on (Date)

OMB No. 1615-0028; Expires 08/31/08

Department of Homeland Security
U.S. Citizenship and Immigration Services

I-600, Petition to Classify Orphan as an Immediate Relative

Instructions

1. Eligibility.

A. Child.

Under immigration law, an orphan is an alien child who has no parents because of the death or disappearance of, abandonment or desertion by, or separation or loss from both parents.

An orphan is also an alien child who has only one parent who is not capable of taking care of the orphan and who has in writing irrevocably released the alien for emigration and adoption.

A petition to classify an alien as an orphan may not be filed on behalf of a child in the United States, unless that child is in parole status and has not been adopted in the United States.

The petition must be filed before the child's 16th birthday.

B. Parent(s).

The petition may be filed by a married U.S. citizen and spouse or unmarried U.S. citizen at least 25 years of age. The spouse does not need to be a U.S. citizen, but must be in lawful immigration status.

C. Adoption abroad.

If the orphan was adopted abroad, it must be established that both the married petitioner and spouse or the unmarried petitioner personally saw and observed the child prior to or during the adoption proceedings. The adoption decree must show that a married petitioner and spouse adopted the child jointly or that an unmarried petitioner was at least 25 years of age at the time of the adoption.

D. Proxy adoption abroad.

If both the petitioner and spouse or the unmarried petitioner did not personally see and observe the child prior to or during the adoption proceedings abroad, the petitioner (and spouse, if married) must submit a statement indicating the petitioner's (and, if married, the spouse's) willingness and intent to readopt the child in the United States.

If requested by USCIS, the petitioner must submit a statement by an official of the State in which the child will reside that readoption is permissible in that State. In addition, evidence of compliance with the preadoption requirements, if any, of that State must be submitted.

E. Preadoption requirements.

If the orphan has not been adopted abroad, the petitioner and spouse or the unmarried petitioner must establish that:

- The child will be adopted in the United States by the petitioner and spouse jointly or by the unmarried petitioner, and that
- The preadoption requirements, if any, of the State of the orphan's proposed residence have been met.

2. Filing Petition for Known Child.

An orphan petition for a child who has been identified must be submitted on a completed Form I-600 with the certification of the petitioner executed and required fee. If the petitioner is married, the Form I-600 must also be signed by the petitioner's spouse.

The petition must be accompanied by the following:

A. Proof of U.S. citizenship of the petitioner.

If a U.S. citizen by birth in the United States, submit a copy of the birth certificate, issued by the civil registrar, vital statistics office or other civil authority. If a birth certificate is not available, submit a statement from the appropriate civil authority certifying that a birth certificate is not available. In such a situation, secondary evidence must be submitted, including:

- **Church records** bearing the seal of the church showing the baptism, dedication or comparable rite occurred within two months after birth and showing the date and place of the petitioner's birth, date of the religious ceremony and the names of the parents;

- **School records** issued by the authority (perferably the first school attended) showing the date of admission to the school, the petitioner's birth date or age at the time, the place of birth and the names of the parents;

- **Census records** (state or federal) showing the name, place of birth, date of birth or age of the petitioner listed;

- **Affidavits** sworn to or affirmed by two persons who were living at the time and who have personal knowledge of the date and place of birth in the United States of the petitioner. Each affidavit should contain the following information regarding the person making the affidavit: his or her full name, address, date and place of birth and relationship to the petitioner, if any, and full information concerning the event and complete details of how the affiant acquired knowledge of petitioner's birth; or

- An unexpired **U.S. passport**, initially issued for ten years may also be submitted as proof of U.S. citizenship.

If the petitioner was born outside the United States, submit a copy of one of the following:

- Certificate of Naturalization or Certificate of Citizenship issued by the U.S. Citizenship and Immigration Services (USCIS) or former Immigration and Naturalization Service (INS);

- Form FS-240, Report of Birth Abroad of a Citizen of the United States, issued by an American embassy;

Form I-600 Instructions (Rev. 10/26/05)Y

- An unexpired U.S. passport initally issued for ten years, or

- An original statement from a U.S. consular officer verifying the applicant's U.S. citizenship with a valid passport.

NOTE: Proof of the lawful immigration status of the petitioner's spouse, if applicable, must be submitted. If the spouse is not a U.S. citizen, proof of the spouse's lawful immigration status, such as Form I-551, Permanent Resident Card; Form I-94, Arrival-Departure Record; or a copy of the biographic pages of the spouse's passport and the nonimmigrant visa pages showing an admission stamp may be submitted.

B. Proof of marriage of petitioner and spouse.

The married petitioner must submit a copy of the certificate of marriage and proof of termination of all prior marriages of himself or herself and spouse. In the case of an unmarried petitioner who was previously married, submit proof of termination of all prior marriages.

NOTE: If any change occurs in the petitioner's marital status while the case is pending, immediately notify the USCIS office where the petition was filed.

C. Proof of age of orphan.

The petitioner should submit a copy of the orphan's birth certificate if obtainable; if not obtainable, submit an explanation together with the best available evidence of birth.

D. Copies of the death certificate(s) of the child's parent(s), if applicable.

E. A certified copy of adoption decree together with certified translation, if the orphan has been lawfully adopted abroad.

F. Evidence that the sole or surviving parent is incapable of providing for the orphan's care and has in writing irrevocably released the orphan for imigration and adoption, if the orphan has only one parent.

G. Evidence that the orphan has been unconditionally abandoned to an orphanage, if the orphan has been placed in an orphanage by his or her parent or parents.

H. Evidence that the preadoption requirements, if any, of the state of the orphan's proposed residence have been met, if the child is to be adopted in the United States.

If is not possible to submit this evidence upon initial filing of the petition under the laws of the State of proposed residence, it may be submitted later. The petition, however, will not be approved without it.

I. Home Study.

The home study must include a statement or attachment recommending or approving the adoption or proposed adoption and be signed by an official of the responsible State agency in the State of the proposed residence or of an agency authorized by that State. In the case of a child adopted abroad, the statement or attachment must be signed by an official of an appropriate public or private adoption agency that is licensed in the United States.

The home study must be prepared by an entity (individual or organization) licensed or otherwise authorized under the law of the State of the orphan's proposed residence to conduct research and preparation for a home study, including the required personal interviews.

If the recommending entity is licensed, the recommendation must state that it is licensed, where it is licensed, its license number, if any, and the period of validity of the license.

However, the research, including the interview and the preparation of the home study, may be done by an individual or group in the United States or abroad that is satisfactory to the recommending entity.

A responsible State agency or licensed agency may accept a home study made by an unlicensed or foreign agency and use that home study as a basis for a favorable recommendation.

The home study must provide an assessment of the capabilities of the prospective adoptive parent(s) to properly parent the orphan and must include a discussion of the following areas:

- An explanation regarding any history of abuse or violence or any complaints, charges, citations, arrests, convictions, prison terms, pardons rehabilitation decrees for breaking or violating any law or ordinance by the petitioner (s) or any additional adult member of the household over age 18.

NOTE: Having committed any crime of moral turpitude or a drug-related offense does not necessarily mean that a petitioner or petitioner's spouse will be found ineligible to adopt an orphan. However, failure to disclose such information may result in denial of this application and/or any subsequent petition for an orphan.

- An assessment of the financial ability of the petitioner and petitioner's spouse, if applicable.

- A detailed description of the living accommodations where the petitioner and petitioner's spouse currently reside(s).

- If the petitioner and petitioner's spouse are residing abroad at the time of the home study, a description of the living accommodations where the child will reside in the United States with the petitioner and petitioner's spouse, if known.

- An assessment of the physical, mental and emotional capabilities of the petitioner and petitioner's spouse in relation to rearing and educating the child.

J. Biometric services.

As part of the USCIS biometric services requirements, the following persons must be fingerprinted in connection with this petition:

- The petitioner and petitioner's spouse, if applicable, and

- Each additional adult member the petitioner's household, 18 years of age or older. **NOTE:** Submit a copy of the birth certificate of each household member over 18.

If necessary, USCIS may also take a photograph and signature of those named above as part of the biometric services.

Petitioners residing in the United States. After filing this petition, USCIS will notify each person in writing of the time and location where they must go to be fingerprinted. Failure to appear to be fingerprinted or for other biometric services may result in denial of the petition.

Petitioners residing abroad. Completed fingerprint cards (Forms FD-258) must be submitted with the petition. Do not bend, fold or crease completed fingerprint cards. Fingerprint cards must be prepared by a U.S. embassy or consulate, USCIS office or military installation.

3. Filing Petition for Known Child Without Full Documentation on Child or Home Study.

When a child has been identified but the documentary evidence relating to the child or the home study is not yet available, an orphan petition may be filed without that evidence or home study.

The evidence outlined in Instructions **2A** and **2B** (proof of petitioner's U.S. citizenship and documentation of marriage of petitioner and spouse), however, must be submitted.

If the necessary evidence relating to the child or the home study is not submitted within one year from the date of submission of the petition, the petition will be considered abandoned and the fee will not be refunded. Any further proceeding will require the filing of a new petition.

4. Submitting Advance Processing Application for Orphan Child Not Yet Identified.

A prospective petitioner may request advance processing when the child has not been identified or when the prospective petitioner and/or spouse is or are going abroad to locate or adopt a child.

If unmarried, the prospective petitioner must be at least 24 years of age, provided that he or she will be at least 25 at the time of the adoption and the completed petition on behalf of a child is filed.

The request must be on Form I-600A, Application for Advance Processing of Orphan Petition, and accompanied by the evidence requested on that form.

After a child or children are located and/or identified, a separate Form I-600 must be filed for each child. If only one Form I-600 is filed, a new fee is not required, provided the form is filed while the advance processing application (Form I-600A) application is pending or within 18 months of the approval of the advance processing application.

5. When Child/Children Are Located and/or Identified.

A separate Form I-600, Petition to Classify Orphan as an Immediate Relative, must be filed for each child.

Generally, Form I-600 should be submitted at the USCIS office where the advance processing application was filed.

If a prospective petitioner goes abroad to adopt or locate a child in one of the countries noted below, he or she should file Form I-600 at the USCIS office having jurisdiction over the place where the child is residing or will be located, unless the case is retained at the stateside office.

USCIS has offices in the following countries: Austria, China, Cuba, the Dominican Republic, El Salvador, Germany, Ghana, Great Britain, Greece, Guatemala, Haiti, Honduras, India, Italy, Jamaica, Kenya, Korea, Mexico, Pakistan, Panama, Peru, the Philippines, Russia, South Africa, Thailand and Vietnam.

If a prospective petitioner goes abroad to any country not listed above to adopt or locate a child he or she should file Form I-600 at the American embassy or consulate having jurisdiction over the place where the child is residing or will be located, unless the case is retained at the Stateside office.

6. General Filing Instructions.

   A. Type or print legibly in black ink.

   B. If extra space is needed to complete any item, attach a continuation sheet, indicate the item number, and date and sign each sheet.

   C. Translations.

   Any foreign language document must be accompanied by a full English translation, that the translator has certified as complete and correct, and by the translator's certification that he or she is competent to translate the foreign language.

   D. Copies.

   If these instructions tell you to submit a copy of a particular document, you do not have to send the original document. However, if there are stamps, remarks, notations, etc., on the back of the original documents, also submit copies of the back of the document(s). You do not have to submit the original document unless USCIS requests it.

   There are times when USCIS must request an original copy of a document. In that case, the original is generally returned after it has been reviewed.

7. Filing the Petition.

A petitioner residing in the United States should send the completed petition to the USCIS office having jurisdiction over his or her place of residence. A petitioner residing outside the United States should consult the nearest American embassy or consulate designated to act on the petition.

8. What Is the Fee?

A fee of **$545.00** must be submitted for filing this petition. However, a fee is not required for this petition if you filed an advance processing application (Form I-600A) within the previous 18 months and it was approved or is still pending.

In addition to the fee for the application, there is a **$70.00** biometric services fee for fingerprinting every adult person living in the household in the United States where the child will reside.

For example, if a petition is filed by a married people residing in the United States with one additional adult member in their household, the total fee that must be submitted would be **$755.00 ($545.00** for the petition and **$210.00** for biometric services for fingerprinting the three adults).

NOTE: If the prospective adoptive parents and any other adult members of the household reside abroad at the time of filing, they are exempt from paying the USCIS biometric services fee. However, they may have to pay the fingerprinting fee charged by the U.S. consular office or military installation.

When more than one petition is submitted by the same petitioner on behalf of orphans who are siblings, only one Form I-600 petition and fee for biometric services is required, unless re-fingerprinting is ordered. If the orphans are not siblings, a separate filing fee must be submitted for each additional Form I-600 petition.

The fee will not be refunded, whether the petition is approved or not. **Do not mail cash.** All checks or money orders, whether U.S. or foreign, must be payable in U.S. currency at a financial institution in the United States. When a check is drawn on the account of a person other than yourself, write your name on the face of the check. If the check is not honored, USCIS will charge you $30.00.

Pay by check or money order in the exact amount. Make the check or money order payable to the **Department of Homeland Security**, unless:

A. You live in Guam, make the check or money order payable to the "Treasurer, Guam" or ;

B. You live in the U.S. Virgin Islands, make your check or money order payable to the "Commissioner of Finance of the Virgin Islands."

How to Check If the Fee Is Correct.

The fee on this form is current as of the edition date appearing in the lower right corner of this page. However, because USCIS fees change periodically, you can verify if the fee is correct by following one of the steps below:

- Visit our website at **www.uscis.gov** and scroll down to "Forms and E-Filing" to check the appropriate fee, or

- Review the Fee Schedule included in your form package, if you called us to request the form, or

- Telephone our National Customer Service Center at **1-800-375-5283** and ask for the fee information.

NOTE: If your petition or application requires a biometric services fee for USCIS to take your fingerprints, photograph or signature, you can use the same procedure above to confirm the biometrics fee.

9. Penalties.

Willful false statements on this form or supporting documents may be punished by fine or imprisonment. U.S. Code, Title 18, Sec. 1001 (formerly Sec. 80.)

10. Authority to Collect Information.

8 USC 1154(a). Routine uses for disclosure under the Privacy Act of 1974 have been published in the Federal Register and are available upon request. USCIS will use the information to determine immigrant eligibility. Submission of the information is voluntary, but failure to provide any or all of the information may result in denial of the petition.

11. USCIS Forms and Information.

To order USCIS forms, call our toll-free number at **1-800-870-3676**. You can also get USCIS forms and information on laws, regulations and procedures by telephoning our National Customer Service Center at **1-800-375-5283** or visiting our internet website at **www.uscis.gov**.

12. Use InfoPass for Appointments.

As an alternative to waiting in line for assistance at your local USCIS office, you can now schedule an appointment through our internet-based system, **InfoPass**. To access the system, visit our website at **www.uscis.gov**. Use the **InfoPass** appointment scheduler and follow the screen prompts to set up your appointment. **InfoPass** generates an electronic appointment notice that appears on the screen. Print the notice and take it with you to your appointment. The notice gives the time and date of your appointment, along with the address of the USCIS office.

13. Reporting Burden.

A person is not required to respond to a collection of information unless it displays a currently valid OMB control number.

Public reporting burden for this collection of information is estimated to average 30 minutes per response, including the time for reviewing instructions, searching existing data sources, gathering and maintaining the data needed, and completing and reviewing the collection of information.

Send comments regarding this burden estimate or any other aspect of this collection of information, including suggestions for reducing this burden, to the: U.S. Citizenship and Immigration Services, Regulatory Management Division, 111 Massachusetts Avenue, N.W., Washington, DC 20529; OMB No. 1615-0028. **Do not mail your completed petition.**

OMB No. 1615-0028; Expires 08/31/08

Department of Homeland Security
U.S. Citizenship and Immigration Services

I-600, Petition to Classify Orphan
as an Immediate Relative

Do not write in this block.	(For USCIS Use Only.)

TO THE SECRETARY OF STATE:
The petition was filed by:

☐ Married petitioner　　　☐ Unmarried petitioner

The petition is approved for orphan:

☐ Adopted abroad　　　☐ Coming to U.S. for adoption.
　　　　　　　　　　　　　Preadoption requirements have been
　　　　　　　　　　　　　met.

Fee Stamp

Remarks:

File number

DATE OF
ACTION

DD

DISTRICT

Type or print legibly in black ink. Complete a separate petition for each child.
Petition is being made to classify the named orphan as an immediate relative

Block I - Information about petitioner.	8. If you are now married, give the following information:

1. My name is: (Last)　(First)　(Middle)

Date and place of present marriage *(mm/dd/yyyy)*

2. Other names used (including maiden name if appropriate):

Name of present spouse (include maiden name of wife)

3. I reside in the U.S. at:　(C/O if appropriate)　(Apt. No.)

Date of birth of spouse *(mm/dd/yyyy)* Place of birth of spouse

　　(Number and Street)　(Town or City)　(State) (Zip Code)

Number of prior marriages of spouse

4. Address Abroad (if any): (Number and Street)　(Apt. No.)

My spouse resides　☐ With me ☐ Apart from me
　　　　　　　　　　　　　　　　　　(provide address below)

　　(Town or city)　(Province)　(Country)

(Apt. No.) (No. and Street)　(City)　(State) (Country)

5. I was born on: *(mm/dd/yyyy)*

9. I am a citizen of the United States through:

☐ Birth　☐ Parents　☐ Naturalization

　　In: (Town or City)　(State or Province)　(Country)

If acquired through naturalization, give name under which naturalized,
number of naturalization certificate, and date and place of naturalization:

6. My telephone number is: (Include Area Code)

7. My marital status is:

☐ Married
☐ Widowed
☐ Divorced
☐ Single
　　☐ I have never been married.
　　☐ I have been previously married _____ time(s).

If not, submit evidence of citizenship. See Instruction **2.a(2).**

If acquired through parentage, have you obtained a certificate in your
own name based on that acquisition?

☐ No　☐ Yes

Have you or any person through whom you claimed citizenship ever lost
U.S. citizenship?

☐ No　☐ Yes (If Yes, attach detailed explanation.)

Received	Trans. In	Ret'd Trans. Out	Completed

Block II - Information about orphan beneficiary.

10. Name at Birth   (First)   (Middle)   (Last)

20. To petitioner's knowledge, does the orphan have any physical or mental affliction?   ☐ Yes   ☐ No

If "Yes," name the affliction.

11. Name at Present (First)   (Middle)   (Last)

12. Any other names by which orphan is or was known.

21. Who has legal custody of the child?

13. Gender   ☐ Male   **14.** Date of birth (mm/dd/yyyy)
        ☐ Female

22. Name of child welfare agency, if any, assisting in this case:

15. Place of Birth (City)   (State or Province)   (Country)

23. Name of attorney abroad, if any, representing petitioner in this case.

16. The beneficiary is an orphan because (check one):
        ☐ He or she has no parents.
        ☐ He or she has only one parent who is the sole or surviving parent.

Address of above.

24. Address in the United States where orphan will reside.

17. If the orphan has only one parent, answer the following:
   a. State what has become of the other parent:

25. Present address of orphan.

   b. Is the remaining parent capable of providing for the orphan's support?   ☐ Yes   ☐ No
   c. Has the remaining parent in writing irrevocably released the orphan for emigration and adoption?   ☐ Yes   ☐ No

25. If orphan is residing in an institution, give full name of institution.

18. Has the orphan been adopted abroad by the petitioner and spouse jointly or the unmarried petitioner?   ☐ Yes   ☐ No

26. If orphan is not residing in an institution, give full name of person with whom orphan is residing.

   If yes, did the petitioner and spouse or unmarried petitioner personally see and observe the child prior to or during the adoption proceedings?   ☐ Yes   ☐ No

27. Give any additional information necessary to locate orphan, such as name of district, section, zone or locality in which orphan resides.

   Date of adoption (mm/dd/yyyy)

   Place of adoption

19. If either answer in Question **18** is "No," answer the following:
   a. Do petitioner and spouse jointly or does the unmarried petitioner intend to adopt the orphan in the United States?
                        ☐ Yes   ☐ No
   b. Have the preadoption requirements, if any, of the orphan's proposed State of residence been met?   ☐ Yes   ☐ No
   c. If **b** is answered "No," will they be met later?
                        ☐ Yes   ☐ No

28. Location of American embassy or consulate where application for visa will be made.
        (City in Foreign Country)   (Foreign Country)

Certification of petitioner.
I certify, under penalty of perjury under the laws of the United States of America, that the foregoing is true and correct and that I will care for an orphan or orphans properly if admitted to the United States.

(Signature of Petitioner)

Executed on (Date)

Certification of married prospective petitioner's spouse.
I certify, under penalty of perjury under the laws of the United States of America, that the foregoing is true and correct and that my spouse and I will care for an orphan or orphans properly if admitted to the United States.

(Signature of Petitioner)

Executed on (Date)

Signature of person preparing form, if other than petitioner.

I declare that this document was prepared by me at the request of the petitioner and is based entirely on information of which I have knowledge.

(Signature)

Street Address and Room or Suite No./City/State/Zip Code

Executed on (Date)

U.S. Department of Justice
Immigration and Naturalization Service

OMB No. 1115-0214

Affidavit of Support Under Section 213A of the Act

INSTRUCTIONS

Purpose of this Form

This form is required to show that an intending immigrant has adequate means of financial support and is not likely to become a public charge.

Sponsor's Obligation

The person completing this affidavit is the sponsor. A sponsor's obligation continues until the sponsored immigrant becomes a U.S. citizen, can be credited with 40 qualifying quarters of work, departs the United States permanently, or dies. Divorce does not terminate the obligation. By signing this form, you, the sponsor, agree to support the intending immigrant and any spouse and/or children immigrating with him or her and to reimburse any government agency or private entity that provides these sponsored immigrants with Federal, State, or local means-tested public benefits.

General Filing Instructions

Please answer all questions by typing or clearly printing in black ink only. Indicate that an item is not applicable with "N/A". If an answer is "none," please so state. If you need extra space to answer any item, attach a sheet of paper with your name and Social Security number, and indicate the number of the item to which the answer refers.

You must submit an affidavit of support for each applicant for immigrant status. You may submit photocopies of this affidavit for any spouse or children immigrating with an immigrant you are sponsoring. For purposes of this form, a spouse or child is immigrating with an immigrant you are sponsoring if he or she is: 1) listed in Part 3 of this affidavit of support; and 2) applies for an immigrant visa or adjustment of status within 6 months of the date this affidavit of support is originally completed and signed. The signature on the affidavit must be notarized by a notary public or signed before an Immigration or a Consular officer.

You should give the completed affidavit of support with all required documentation to the sponsored immigrant for submission to either a Consular Officer with Form OF-230, Application for Immigrant Visa and Alien Registration, or an Immigration Officer with Form I-485, Application to Register Permanent Residence or Adjust Status. You may enclose the affidavit of support and accompanying documents in a sealed envelope to be opened only by the designated Government official. The sponsored immigrant must submit the affidavit of support to the Government within 6 months of its signature.

Who Needs an Affidavit of Support under Section 213A?

This affidavit must be filed at the time an intending immigrant is applying for an immigrant visa or adjustment of status. It is required for:

- All immediate relatives, including orphans, and family-based immigrants. (Self-petitioning widow/ers and battered spouses and children are exempt from this requirement); and

- Employment-based immigrants where a relative filed the immigrant visa petition or has a significant ownership interest (5 percent or more) in the entity that filed the petition.

Who Completes an Affidavit of Support under Section 213A?

- For immediate relatives and family-based immigrants, the family member petitioning for the intending immigrant must be the sponsor.

- For employment-based immigrants, the petitioning relative or a relative with a significant ownership interest (5 percent or more) in the petitioning entity must be the sponsor. The term "relative," for these purposes, is defined as husband, wife, father, mother, child, adult son or daughter, brother, or sister.

- If the petitioner cannot meet the income requirements, a joint sponsor may submit an additional affidavit of support.

A sponsor, or joint sponsor, must also be:

- A citizen or national of the United States or an alien lawfully admitted to the United States for permanent residence;

- At least 18 years of age; and

- Domiciled in the United States or its territories and possessions.

Sponsor's Income Requirement

As a sponsor, your household income must equal or exceed 125 percent of the Federal poverty line for your household size. For the purpose of the affidavit of support, household size includes yourself, all persons related to you by birth, marriage, or adoption living in your residence, your dependents, any immigrants you have previously sponsored using INS Form I-864 if that obligation has not terminated, and the intending immigrant(s) in Part 3 of this affidavit of support. The poverty guidelines are calculated and published annually by the Department of Health and Human Services. Sponsors who are on active duty in the U.S. Armed Forces other than for training need only demonstrate income at 100 percent of the poverty line *if* they are submitting this affidavit for the purpose of sponsoring their spouse or child.

If you are currently employed and have an *individual* income which meets or exceeds 125 percent of the Federal poverty line or (100 percent, if applicable) for your household size, you do not need to list the income of any other person. When determining your income, you may include the income generated by individuals related to you by birth, marriage, or adoption who are living in your residence, if they have lived in your residence for the previous 6 months, or who are listed as dependents on your most recent Federal income tax return whether or not they live in your residence. For their income to be considered, these household members or dependents must be willing to make their income available for the support of the sponsored immigrant(s) if necessary, and to complete and sign Form I-864A, Contract Between Sponsor and Household Member. However, a household member who is the immigrant you are sponsoring only need complete Form I-864A if his or her income will be used to determine your ability to support a spouse and/or children immigrating with him or her.

If in any of the most recent 3 tax years, you and your spouse each reported income on a joint income tax return, but you want to use only your own income to qualify (and your spouse is not submitting a Form I-864A), you may provide a separate breakout of your individual income for these years. Your individual income will be based on the earnings from your W-2 forms, Wage and Tax Statement, submitted to IRS for any such years. If necessary to meet the income requirement, you may also submit evidence of other income listed on your tax returns which can be attributed to you. You must provide documentation of such reported income, including Forms 1099 sent by the payer, which show your name and Social Security number.

You must calculate your household size and total household income as indicated in Parts 4.B. and 4.C. of this form. You must compare your total household income with the minimum income requirement for your household size using the poverty guidelines. For the purposes of the affidavit of support, determination of your ability to meet the income requirements will be based on the most recent poverty guidelines published in the Federal Register at the time the Consular or Immigration Officer makes a decision on the intending immigrant's application for an immigrant visa or adjustment of status. Immigration and Consular Officers will begin to use updated poverty guidelines on the first day of the second month after the date the guidelines are published in the Federal Register.

If your total household income is equal to or higher than the minimum income requirement for your household size, you do not need to provide information on your assets, and you may *not* have a joint sponsor unless you are requested to do so by a Consular or Immigration Officer. If your total household income does not meet the minimum income requirement, the intending immigrant will be ineligible for an immigrant visa or adjustment of status, unless:

- You provide evidence of assets that meet the requirements outlined under "Evidence of Assets" below; and/or

- The immigrant you are sponsoring provides evidence of assets that meet the requirements under "Evidence of Assets" below; or

- A joint sponsor assumes the liability of the intending immigrant with you. A joint sponsor must execute a separate affidavit of support on behalf of the intending

immigrant and any accompanying family members. A joint sponsor must individually meet the minimum requirement of 125 percent of the poverty line based on his or her household size and income and/or assets, including any assets of the sponsored immigrant.

The Government may pursue verification of any information provided on or in support of this form, including employment, income, or assets with the employer, financial or other institutions, the Internal Revenue Service, or the Social Security Administration.

Evidence of Income

In order to complete this form you must submit the following evidence of income:

- A copy of your complete Federal income tax return, as filed with the Internal Revenue Service, for each of the most recent 3 tax years. If you were not required to file a tax return in any of the most recent 3 tax years, you must provide an explanation. If you filed a joint income tax return and are using only your own income to qualify, you must also submit copies of your W-2s for each of the most recent 3 tax years, and if necessary to meet the income requirement, evidence of other income reported on your tax returns, such as Forms 1099.

- If you rely on income of any members of your household or dependents in order to reach the minimum income requirement, copies of their Federal income tax returns for the most recent 3 tax years. These persons must each complete and sign a Form I-864A, Contract Between Sponsor and Household Member.

- Evidence of current employment or self-employment, such as a recent pay statement, or a statement from your employer on business stationery, showing beginning date of employment, type of work performed, and salary or wages paid. You must also provide evidence of current employment for any person whose income is used to qualify.

Evidence of Assets

If you want to use your assets, the assets of your household members or dependents, and/or the assets of the immigrant you are sponsoring to meet the minimum income requirement, you must provide evidence of assets with a cash value that equals at least five times the difference between your total household income and the minimum income requirement. For the assets of a household member, other than the immigrant(s) you are sponsoring, to be considered, the household member must complete and sign Form I-864A, Contract Between Sponsor and Household Member.

All assets must be supported with evidence to verify location, ownership, and value of each asset. Any liens and liabilities relating to the assets must be documented. List only assets that can be readily converted into cash within one year. Evidence of assets includes, but is not limited to the following:

- Bank statements covering the last 12 months, *or* a statement from an officer of the bank or other financial institution in which you have deposits, including deposit/withdrawal history for the last 12 months, and current balance;

- Evidence of ownership and value of stocks, bonds, and certificates of deposit, and date(s) acquired;

- Evidence of ownership and value of other personal property, and date(s) acquired; and

- Evidence of ownership and value of any real estate, and date(s) acquired.

Change of Sponsor's Address

You are required by 8 U.S.C. 1183a(d) and 8 CFR 213a.3 to report every change of address to the Immigration and Naturalization Service and the State(s) in which the sponsored immigrant(s) reside(s). You must report changes of address to INS on Form I-865, Sponsor's Notice of Change of Address, within 30 days of any change of address. You must also report any change in your address to the State(s) in which the sponsored immigrant(s) live.

Penalties

If you include in this affidavit of support any material information that you know to be false, you may be liable for criminal prosecution under the laws of the United States.

If you fail to give notice of your change of address, as required by 8 U.S.C. 1183a(d) and 8 CFR 213a.3, you may be liable for the civil penalty established by 8 U.S.C. 1183a(d)(2). The amount of the civil penalty will depend on whether you failed to give this notice because you were aware that the immigrant(s) you sponsored had received Federal, State, or local means-tested public benefits.

Privacy Act Notice

Authority for the collection of the information requested on this form is contained in 8 U.S.C. 1182(a)(4), 1183a, 1184(a), and 1258. The information will be used principally by the INS or by any Consular Officer to whom it is furnished, to support an alien's application for benefits under the Immigration and Nationality Act and specifically the assertion that he or she has adequate means of financial support and will not become a public charge. Submission of the information is voluntary. Failure to provide the information will result in denial of the application for an immigrant visa or adjustment of status.

The information may also, as a matter of routine use, be disclosed to other Federal, State, and local agencies or private entities providing means-tested public benefits for use in civil action against the sponsor for breach of contract. It may also be disclosed as a matter of routine use to other Federal, State, local, and foreign law enforcement and regulatory agencies to enable these entities to carry out their law enforcement responsibilites.

Reporting Burden

A person is not required to respond to a collection of information unless it displays a currently valid OMB control number. We try to create forms and instructions that are accurate, can be easily understood, and which impose the least possible burden on you to provide us with information. Often this is difficult because some immigration laws are very complex. The reporting burden for this collection of information on Form I-864 is computed as follows: 1) learning about the form, 63 minutes; 2) completing the form, 105 minutes; and 3) assembling and filing the form, 65 minutes, for an estimated average of 3 hours and 48 minutes minutes per response. The reporting burden for collection of information on Form I-864A is computed as: 1) learning about the form, 20 minutes; 2) completing the form, 55 minutes; 3) assembling and filing the form, 30 minutes, for an estimated average of 1 hour and 45 minutes per response. If you have comments regarding the accuracy of this estimates, or suggestions for making this form simpler, you can write to the Immigration and Naturalization Service, HQPDI, 425 I Street, N.W., Room 4034, Washington, DC 20536. **DO NOT MAIL YOUR COMPLETED AFFIDAVIT OF SUPPORT TO THIS ADDRESS.**

CHECK LIST

The following items must be submitted with Form I-864, Affidavit of Support Under Section 213A:

For *ALL* sponsors:

☐ This form, the **I-864, completed and signed** before a notary public or a Consular or Immigration Officer.

☐ Proof of **current employment** or self employment.

☐ Your individual Federal **income tax returns for the most recent 3 tax years,** or an explanation if fewer are submitted. Your **W-2s** for any of the most recent 3 tax years for which you filed a joint tax return but are using only your own income to qualify. Forms 1099 or evidence of other reported income *if* necessary to qualify.

For *SOME* sponsors:

☐ *If the immigrant you are sponsoring is bringing a spouse or children,* **photocopies of the immigrant's affidavit of support** for each spouse and/or child immigrating with the immigrant you are sponsoring.

☐ *If you are on active duty in the U.S. Armed Forces and are sponsoring a spouse or child using the 100 percent of poverty level exception,* **proof of your active military status.**

If you are using the income of persons in your household or dependents to qualify,

☐ A separate **Form I-864A** for each person whose income you will use. A sponsored immigrant/household member who is not immigrating with a spouse and/or child **does not need to complete Form I-864A.**

☐ Proof of their **residency and relationship** to you if they are not listed as dependents on your income tax return for the most recent tax year.

☐ Proof of their **current employment** or self-employment.

☐ Copies of their individual Federal **income tax returns for the 3 most recent tax years,** or an explanation if fewer are submitted.

If you use your assets or the assets of the sponsored immigrant to qualify,

☐ **Documentation of assets** establishing location, ownership, date of acquisition, and value. Evidence of any liens or liabilities against these assets.

☐ A separate **Form I-864A** for each household member other than the sponsored immigrant/household member.

If you are a joint sponsor or the relative of an employment-based immigrant requiring an affidavit of support, **proof of your citizenship status.**

☐ For U.S. citizens or nationals, a copy of your birth certificate, passport, or certificate of naturalization or citizenship.

☐ For lawful permanent residents, a copy of both sides of your I-551, Permanent Resident Card.

OMB No. 1115-0214

U.S. Department of Justice
Immigration and Naturalization Service

Affidavit of Support Under Section 213A of the Act

START HERE - Please Type or Print

Part 1. Information on Sponsor (You)

Last Name	First Name	Middle Name

Mailing Address *(Street Number and Name)*	Apt/Suite Number

City	State or Province

Country	ZIP/Postal Code	Telephone Number

Place of Residence if different from above *(Street Number and Name)*	Apt/Suite Number

City	State or Province

Country	ZIP/Postal Code	Telephone Number

Date of Birth *(Month, Day, Year)*	Place of Birth *(City, State, Country)*	Are you a U.S. Citizen? ☐ Yes ☐ No

Social Security Number	A-Number *(If any)*

FOR AGENCY USE ONLY

This Affidavit

[ ] Meets

[ ] Does not meet

Requirements of Section 213A

Receipt

Officer or I.J. Signature

Location

Date

Part 2. Basis for Filing Affidavit of Support

I am filing this affidavit of support because *(check one)*:

a. ☐ I filed/am filing the alien relative petition.

b. ☐ I filed/am filing an alien worker petition on behalf of the intending

immigrant, who is related to me as my _____ .
(relationship)

c. ☐ I have ownership interest of at least 5% _____ .
(name of entity which filed visa petition)

which filed an alien worker petition on behalf of the intending

immigrant, who is related to me as my _____ .
(relationship)

d. ☐ I am a joint sponsor willing to accept the legal obligations with any other sponsor(s).

Part 3. Information on the Immigrant(s) You Are Sponsoring

Last Name	First Name	Middle Name

Date of Birth *(Month, Day, Year)*	Sex ☐ Male ☐ Female	Social Security Number *(If any)*

Country of Citizenship	A-Number *(If any)*

Current Address *(Street Number and Name)*	Apt/Suite Number	City

State/Province	Country	ZIP/Postal Code	Telephone Number

List any spouse and/or children immigrating with the immigrant named above in this Part: *(Use additional sheet of paper if necessary.)*

Name	Relationship to Sponsored Immigrant			Date of Birth			A-Number *(If any)*	Social Security *(If any)*
	Spouse	Son	Daughter	Mo.	Day	Yr.		

Form I-864 (Rev. 11/05/01)Y

ScriptObject

Part 4. Eligibility to Sponsor

To be a sponsor you must be a U.S. citizen or national or a lawful permanent resident. If you are not the petitioning relative, you must provide proof of status. To prove status, U.S. citizens or nationals must attach a copy of a document proving status, such as a U.S. passport, birth certificate, or certificate of naturalization, and lawful permanent residents must attach a copy of both sides of their Permanent Resident Card (Form I-551).

The determination of your eligibility to sponsor an immigrant will be based on an evaluation of your demonstrated ability to maintain an annual income at or above 125 percent of the Federal poverty line (100 percent if you are a petitioner sponsoring your spouse or child and you are on active duty in the U.S. Armed Forces). The assessment of your ability to maintain an adequate income will include your current employment, household size, and household income as shown on the Federal income tax returns for the 3 most recent tax years. Assets that are readily converted to cash and that can be made available for the support of sponsored immigrants if necessary, including any such assets of the immigrant(s) you are sponsoring, may also be considered.

The greatest weight in determining eligibility will be placed on current employment and household income. If a petitioner is unable to demonstrate ability to meet the stated income and asset requirements, a joint sponsor who *can* meet the income and asset requirements is needed. Failure to provide adequate evidence of income and/or assets or an affidavit of support completed by a joint sponsor will result in denial of the immigrant's application for an immigrant visa or adjustment to permanent resident status.

A. Sponsor's Employment

I am: 1. ☐ Employed by _____ *(Provide evidence of employment)*

Annual salary _____ or hourly wage $ _____ *(for _____ hours per week)*

2. ☐ Self employed _____ *(Name of business)*

Nature of employment or business _____

3. ☐ Unemployed or retired since _____

B. Sponsor's Household Size

Number

1. Number of persons (related to you by birth, marriage, or adoption) living in your residence, including yourself *(Do NOT include persons being sponsored in this affidavit.)* _____

2. Number of immigrants being sponsored in this affidavit. *(Include all persons in Part 3.)* _____

3. Number of immigrants **NOT** living in your household whom you are obligated to support under a previously signed Form I-864. _____

4. Number of persons who are otherwise dependent on you, as claimed in your tax return for the most recent tax year. _____

5. Total household size. *(Add lines 1 through 4.)* **Total** _____

List persons below who are included in lines 1 or 3 for whom you previously have submitted INS Form I-864, *if your support obligation has not terminated.*

(If additional space is needed, use additional paper)

Name	A-Number	Date Affidavit of Support Signed	Relationship

Part 4.   **Eligibility to Sponsor**   *(Continued)*

C. Sponsor's Annual Household Income

Enter total unadjusted income from your Federal income tax return for the most recent tax year below. If you last filed a joint income tax return but are using only your *own* income to qualify, list total earnings from your W-2 Forms, or, *if* necessary to reach the required income for your household size, include income from other sources listed on your tax return. If your *individual* income does not meet the income requirement for your household size, you may also list total income for anyone related to you by birth, marriage, or adoption currently living with you in your residence if they have lived in your residence for the previous 6 months, or any person shown as a dependent on your Federal income tax return for the most recent tax year, even if not living in the household. For their income to be considered, household members or dependents must be willing to make their income available for support of the sponsored immigrant(s) and to complete and sign Form I-864A, Contract Between Sponsor and Household Member. A sponsored immigrant/household member only need complete Form I-864A if his or her income will be used to determine your ability to support a spouse and/or children immigrating with him or her.

You must attach evidence of current employment and copies of income tax returns as filed with the IRS for the most recent 3 tax years for yourself and all persons whose income is listed below. See "Required Evidence " in Instructions. Income from all 3 years will be considered in determining your ability to support the immigrant(s) you are sponsoring.

☐ I filed a single/separate tax return for the most recent tax year.

☐ I filed a joint return for the most recent tax year which includes only my own income.

☐ I filed a joint return for the most recent tax year which includes income for my spouse and myself.

  ☐ I am submitting documentation of my individual income (Forms W-2 and 1099).

  ☐ I am qualifying using my spouse's income; my spouse is submitting a Form I-864A.

Indicate most recent tax year	_____
	(tax year)
Sponsor's individual income	$ _____
or	
Sponsor and spouse's combined income *(If spouse's income is to be considered, spouse must submit Form I-864A.)*	$ _____
Income of other qualifying persons. *(List names; include spouse if applicable. Each person must complete Form I-864A.)*	
_____	$ _____
_____	$ _____
_____	$ _____
Total Household Income	$ _____

Explain on separate sheet of paper if you or any of the above listed individuals were not required to file Federal income tax returns for the most recent 3 years, or if other explanation of income, employment, or evidence is necessary.

D. Determination of Eligibility Based on Income

1. ☐ I am subject to the 125 percent of poverty line requirement for sponsors.
     ☐ I am subject to the 100 percent of poverty line requirement for sponsors on active duty in the U.S. Armed Forces sponsoring their spouse or child.
2.   Sponsor's total household size, from Part 4.B., line 5   _____ .
3.   Minimum income requirement from the Poverty Guidelines chart for the year of   _____ is $ _____
       for this household size.   *(year)*

If you are currently employed and your household income for your household size is equal to or greater than the applicable poverty line requirement (from line D.3.), you do not need to list assets (Parts 4.E. and 5) or have a joint sponsor (Part 6) unless you are requested to do so by a Consular or Immigration Officer. You may skip to Part 7, Use of the Affidavit of Support to Overcome Public Charge Ground of Admissibility. **Otherwise, you should continue with Part 4.E.**

Part 4.   Eligibility to Sponsor   *(Continued)*

E. Sponsor's Assets and Liabilities

Your assets and those of your qualifying household members and dependents may be used to demonstrate ability to maintain an income at or above 125 percent (or 100 percent, if applicable) of the poverty line *if* they are available for the support of the sponsored immigrant(s) and can readily be converted into cash within 1 year. The household member, other than the immigrant(s) you are sponsoring, must complete and sign Form I-864A, Contract Between Sponsor and Household Member. List the cash value of each asset *after* any debts or liens are subtracted. Supporting evidence must be attached to establish location, ownership, date of acquisition, and value of each asset listed, including any liens and liabilities related to each asset listed. See "Evidence of Assets" in Instructions.

Type of Asset	Cash Value of Assets *(Subtract any debts)*
Savings deposits	$
Stocks, bonds, certificates of deposit	$
Life insurance cash value	$
Real estate	$
Other *(specify)*	$
Total Cash Value of Assets	$ _____

Part 5.   Immigrant's Assets and Offsetting Liabilities

The sponsored immigrant's assets may also be used in support of your ability to maintain income at or above 125 percent of the poverty line *if* the assets are or will be available in the United States for the support of the sponsored immigrant(s) and can readily be converted into cash within 1 year.

The sponsored immigrant should provide information on his or her assets in a format similar to part 4.E. above. Supporting evidence must be attached to establish location, ownership, and value of each asset listed, including any liens and liabilities for each asset listed. See "Evidence of Assets" in Instructions.

Part 6.   Joint Sponsors

If household income and assets do not meet the appropriate poverty line for your household size, a joint sponsor is required. There may be more than one joint sponsor, but each joint sponsor must individually meet the 125 percent of poverty line requirement based on his or her household income and/or assets, including any assets of the sponsored immigrant(s). By submitting a separate Affidavit of Support under Section 213A of the Act (Form I-864), a joint sponsor accepts joint responsibility with the petitioner for the sponsored immigrant(s) until they become U.S. citizens, can be credited with 40 quarters of work, leave the United States permanently, or die.

Part 7.   Use of the Affidavit of Support to Overcome Public Charge Ground of Inadmissibility

Section 212(a)(4)(C) of the Immigration and Nationality Act provides that an alien seeking permanent residence as an immediate relative (including an orphan), as a family-sponsored immigrant, or as an alien who will accompany or follow to join another alien is considered to be likely to become a public charge and is inadmissible to the United States unless a sponsor submits a legally enforceable affidavit of support on behalf of the alien. Section 212(a)(4)(D) imposes the same requirement on an employment-based immigrant, and those aliens who accompany or follow to join the employment- based immigrant, if the employment-based immigrant will be employed by a relative, or by a firm in which a relative owns a significant interest. Separate affidavits of support are required for family members at the time they immigrate if they are not included on this affidavit of support or do not apply for an immigrant visa or adjustment of status within 6 months of the date this affidavit of support is originally signed. The sponsor must provide the sponsored immigrant(s) whatever support is necessary to maintain them at an income that is at least 125 percent of the Federal poverty guidelines.

> *I submit this affidavit of support in consideration of the sponsored immigrant(s) not being found inadmissible to the United States under section 212(a)(4)(C) (or 212(a)(4)(D) for an employment-based immigrant) and to enable the sponsored immigrant(s) to overcome this ground of inadmissibility. I agree to provide the sponsored immigrant(s) whatever support is necessary to maintain the sponsored immigrant(s) at an income that is at least 125 percent of the Federal poverty guidelines. I understand that my obligation will continue until my death or the sponsored immigrant(s) have become U.S. citizens, can be credited with 40 quarters of work, depart the United States permanently, or die.*

Part 7.   Use of the Affidavit of Support to Overcome Public Charge Grounds   *(Continued)*

Notice of Change of Address.

Sponsors are required to provide written notice of any change of address within 30 days of the change in address until the sponsored immigrant(s) have become U.S. citizens, can be credited with 40 quarters of work, depart the United States permanently, or die. To comply with this requirement, the sponsor must complete INS Form I-865. Failure to give this notice may subject the sponsor to the civil penalty established under section 213A(d)(2) which ranges from $250 to $2,000, unless the failure to report occurred with the knowledge that the sponsored immigrant(s) had received means-tested public benefits, in which case the penalty ranges from $2,000 to $5,000.

If my address changes for any reason before my obligations under this affidavit of support terminate, I will complete and file INS Form I-865, Sponsor's Notice of Change of Address, within 30 days of the change of address. I understand that failure to give this notice may subject me to civil penalties.

Means-tested Public Benefit Prohibitions and Exceptions.

Under section 403(a) of Public Law 104-193 (Welfare Reform Act), aliens lawfully admitted for permanent residence in the United States, with certain exceptions, are ineligible for most Federally-funded means-tested public benefits during their first 5 years in the United States. This provision does not apply to public benefits specified in section 403(c) of the Welfare Reform Act or to State public benefits, including emergency Medicaid; short-term, non-cash emergency relief; services provided under the National School Lunch and Child Nutrition Acts; immunizations and testing and treatment for communicable diseases; student assistance under the Higher Education Act and the Public Health Service Act; certain forms of foster-care or adoption assistance under the Social Security Act; Head Start programs; means-tested programs under the Elementary and Secondary Education Act; and Job Training Partnership Act programs.

Consideration of Sponsor's Income in Determining Eligibility for Benefits.

If a permanent resident alien is no longer statutorily barred from a Federally-funded means-tested public benefit program and applies for such a benefit, the income and resources of the sponsor and the sponsor's spouse will be considered (or deemed) to be the income and resources of the sponsored immigrant in determining the immigrant's eligibility for Federal means-tested public benefits. Any State or local government may also choose to consider (or deem) the income and resources of the sponsor and the sponsor's spouse to be the income and resources of the immigrant for the purposes of determining eligibility for their means-tested public benefits. The attribution of the income and resources of the sponsor and the sponsor's spouse to the immigrant will continue until the immigrant becomes a U.S. citizen or has worked or can be credited with 40 qualifying quarters of work, provided that the immigrant or the worker crediting the quarters to the immigrant has not received any Federal means-tested public benefit during any creditable quarter for any period after December 31, 1996.

I understand that, under section 213A of the Immigration and Nationality Act (the Act), as amended, this affidavit of support constitutes a contract between me and the U.S. Government. This contract is designed to protect the United States Government, and State and local government agencies or private entities that provide means-tested public benefits, from having to pay benefits to or on behalf of the sponsored immigrant(s), for as long as I am obligated to support them under this affidavit of support. I understand that the sponsored immigrants, or any Federal, State, local, or private entity that pays any means-tested benefit to or on behalf of the sponsored immigrant(s), are entitled to sue me if I fail to meet my obligations under this affidavit of support, as defined by section 213A and INS regulations.

Civil Action to Enforce.

If the immigrant on whose behalf this affidavit of support is executed receives any Federal, State, or local means-tested public benefit before this obligation terminates, the Federal, State, or local agency or private entity may request reimbursement from the sponsor who signed this affidavit. If the sponsor fails to honor the request for reimbursement, the agency may sue the sponsor in any U.S. District Court or any State court with jurisdiction of civil actions for breach of contract. INS will provide names, addresses, and Social Security account numbers of sponsors to benefit-providing agencies for this purpose. Sponsors may also be liable for paying the costs of collection, including legal fees.

Part 7. **Use of the Affidavit of Support to Overcome Public Charge Grounds** *(Continued)*

I acknowledge that section 213A(a)(1)(B) of the Act grants the sponsored immigrant(s) and any Federal, State, local, or private agency that pays any means-tested public benefit to or on behalf of the sponsored immigrant(s) standing to sue me for failing to meet my obligations under this affidavit of support. I agree to submit to the personal jurisdiction of any court of the United States or of any State, territory, or possession of the United States if the court has subject matter jurisdiction of a civil lawsuit to enforce this affidavit of support. I agree that no lawsuit to enforce this affidavit of support shall be barred by any statute of limitations that might otherwise apply, so long as the plaintiff initiates the civil lawsuit no later than ten (10) years after the date on which a sponsored immigrant last received any means-tested public benefits.

Collection of Judgment.

I acknowledge that a plaintiff may seek specific performance of my support obligation. Furthermore, any money judgment against me based on this affidavit of support may be collected through the use of a judgment lien under 28 U.S.C 3201, a writ of execution under 28 U.S.C 3203, a judicial installment payment order under 28 U.S.C 3204, garnishment under 28 U.S.C 3205, or through the use of any corresponding remedy under State law. I may also be held liable for costs of collection, including attorney fees.

Concluding Provisions.

I, _____ , certify under penalty of perjury under the laws of the United States that:

> *(a) I know the contents of this affidavit of support signed by me;*
>
> *(b) All the statements in this affidavit of support are true and correct,*
>
> *(c) I make this affidavit of support for the consideration stated in Part 7, freely, and without any mental reservation or purpose of evasion;*
>
> *(d) Income tax returns submitted in support of this affidavit are true copies of the returns filed with the Internal Revenue Service; and*
>
> *(e) Any other evidence submitted is true and correct.*

_____   _____
(Sponsor's Signature)   *(Date)*

Subscribed and sworn to (or affirmed) before me this

_____ day of _____ , _____
                                (Month)   *(Year)*

at _____ .

My commission expires on _____ .

_____
(Signature of Notary Public or Officer Administering Oath)

_____
(Title)

Part 8. **If someone other than the sponsor prepared this affidavit of support, that person must complete the following:**

I certify under penalty of perjury under the laws of the United States that I prepared this affidavit of support at the sponsor's request, and that this affidavit of support is based on all information of which I have knowledge.

Signature	Print Your Name	Date	Daytime Telephone Number

Firm Name and Address

Chapter 7

Independent Adoptions

It is possible to do an adoption without working with an agency. These types of adoptions are called parent-initiated, private, or independent adoptions. The adoptive parents locate a birth mother on their own (or with the help of a professional adoption facilitator or attorney), without help from an adoption agency. Some singles and couples find that this method of adoption is better suited to their needs. The benefits of parent-initiated adoptions are that:

- ☑ You can adopt a newborn.

- ☑ You do not have to work with an agency.

- ☑ You have direct control over the adoption process.

- ☑ You choose the birth mother yourself.

- ☑ There is more personal contact with the birth mother.

- ☑ There is no application process or waiting periods.

Another important benefit of independent adoption is that you can avoid any potential prejudice you might find at an agency. Instead of convincing other people you should be able to adopt, you're on the front lines, looking for a birth mother. You can locate a birth mother whom you are certain has no problem with your sexual orientation. You don't have to hide who you are in an independent adoption.

While these benefits sound good, there are disadvantages, too. If you go through the adoption process without an agency, you may not be completely aware of all the laws and regulations you need to comply with (although an experienced attorney can help you here). There is also always the chance that the birth mother will change her mind. While this can happen with agency adoptions as well, the chance of it increases when an agency is not involved to counsel and support the birth mother in making the placement decision. And when you work with an agency, if the birth mother changes her mind, there are other babies available, so you don't start over from scratch. An agency can also often provide an experienced hand that will guide your adoption and help you get over any bumps in the road because their business is helping adoptions happen.

Parent-initiated adoption (that is, nonagency adoption) is not permitted in Colorado, Connecticut, Delaware, Massachusetts, and Wisconsin. In these states you must use an agency for the adoption process, but this doesn't mean you can't locate a birth mother on your own and then have the adoption handled by an agency (see the following section).

Adopting Independently With an Agency

Many parents who choose to locate a birth mother on their own do use an agency for the actual adoption process itself. If you're interested in doing this, you need to interview agencies in your area and choose one that will handle a parent-initiated adoption. The agency will coordinate the home study, provide counseling, and work with your attorney to complete the adoption process. If you are comfortable working with an agency in this way, it can make the entire process go much more smoothly. There is an intermediary between you and the birth mother and you have someone handling the paperwork on your behalf. You've done the important part—selecting the birth mother—you can then rely on the agency to handle the paperwork and the agency can also step in and help should any problems arise.

The agency will usually handle payment of the birth mother's expenses so you don't have to pay them directly (it will be part of the costs you are required to pay to the agency). However, you will have to pay an agency fee, which you would not pay if you had handled the adoption directly with the birth mother.

> For support and information, contact Families for Private Adoption, at *www.ffpa.org*.

Finding a Birth Mother on Your Own

There are several ways to go about finding a birth mother on your own. First, you need to talk to an attorney who is experienced in handling adoptions. Not only will the attorney help you understand the law and how you should go about contacting and reaching an agreement with a birth mother (there are laws you must follow), but additionally, many experienced adoption attorneys have contact with birth mothers who are seeking adoptive parents to place their babies with and may be able to help you find a birth mother.

Word of mouth is another excellent way to locate a birth mother. Tell your friends and family about your search and ask them to keep their ears open for you. Mention your search to coworkers and acquaintances. Some adoptive parents have business cards made up with their name, number, and a brief description along with words to the effect of "I/We can provide a loving home for your baby. Please call us." Hand these out to friends and family and ask them to pass them along to anyone who might be interested. If you belong to a church or synagogue, that is a good place to pass them out. Post them on a bulletin board or ask to have it mentioned in a newsletter.

Other potential parents create a letter that is addressed to prospective birth mothers. This is often called a "Dear Birth Mother" letter, and describes you and your hopes to have a family. This is a good way to let a birth mother know about you before she has to pick up the phone and call you. There are many Websites where you can post information about yourself for potential birth mothers. You can also post these letters at pregnancy counseling services and give them to adoption attorneys to post in their offices. Do a search for "dear birth mother" and you will find many you can consider. You may also wish to create your own Website and include the URL on business cards, in birth mother letters, and in any posts to message boards that you make. You can post photos of you, your home, your neighborhood, your pets, and more, on the site and include as much information about yourself as you would like.

Facilitators

If you have no idea where to look to find a birth mother, but do not want to work with an agency, another option is to use an adoption facilitator. This is a professional who works to bring birth mothers and adoptive parents together. Facilitators are not licensed in most states and some states do not allow the use of facilitators. It is a good idea to speak with your attorney before approaching a facilitator to make sure it is legal in your state and to understand the limitations. If you do decide to work with a facilitator:

◪ Check his or her references carefully.

◪ Find out how many babies he placed in total, as well as in the last year.

◪ Be clear on any fees involved, as well as what the fees would be if a birth mother changes her mind.

◪ Get a contract in writing and have it reviewed by your attorney.

◪ Ask how the facilitator finds potential birth mothers.

◪ Question the facilitator's background and look for one who is an experienced social worker or adoption counselor.

States that permit payments to facilitators:

◪ California

◪ Connecticut

◪ Florida

◪ Iowa

States that do not permit the use of a facilitator:

- Alabama

- Colorado

- Delaware

- District of Columbia

- Illinois

- Kentucky

- Louisiana

- Maryland

- Massachusetts

- Michigan

- Nevada

- New Jersey

- New York

- North Carolina

- North Dakota

- Oklahoma

- Oregon

- Tennessee

- Texas

- Vermont

- Virginia

- West Virginia

- Wisconsin

Other states have no specific laws allowing or disallowing the use of a facilitator, so if you use one and for some reason end up in court, it is unclear how the courts will handle it until there is a test case in your state.

When choosing a facilitator, you should contact your state adoption specialist and ask if there have been any complaints filed against facilitators you are considering.

Advertising

If want to locate a birth mother on your own, you will probably want to do some advertising. You may have seen classified ads in your local paper or in national papers with potential adoptive parents seeking birth mothers. Before you place an ad, talk with your attorney about your state's laws. Some states do not permit any advertising, and some states have restrictions.

States that do not permit advertising by prospective parents include:

- Alabama

- California

- Delaware

- Florida

- Georgia

- Idaho

- Kansas

- Kentucky

- Maine

- Massachusetts

- Nevada

- North Carolina

- Ohio

- Washington

Study some ads to get a feeling for what they are like and what appeals to you. Note that if your ad starts with the letter A, that it will be near the top of all the adoption ads in the paper it is in (because the ads appear in alphabetical order). Because most classifieds are short, you will want to spend a lot of time polishing your ad so that it contains the most information in the clearest way. Most ads make references to a loving home, financial stability, friendly neighborhoods, church, close-knit family, and other positive factors. Mentioning your profession can help if it is prestigious or comforting sounding (such as a doctor, lawyer, nurse, or teacher). It's up to you if you want to mention you are gay. Some parents feel they want to be up front about this from the beginning, while others fear it might scare away some birth mothers who, once they got to know you, would not mind. If you have created a Website, you may wish to include the URL in the ad (for this reason it's important to have a Website with a short URL if at all possible).

When considering a print ad, find out what the paper's circulation is and notice how many adoption ads they have (if they have a lot it may mean a lot of birth mothers look there, but it could also mean your ad will get lost). Before you place an online ad, make sure you find out how many hits the site receives each month and ask for references. Be wary of inflated fees for ads.

Choosing a Birth Mother

Choosing a birth mother is a delicate process. It's exciting and terrifying at the same time. When a birth mother contacts you, your first reaction might be to finalize things before she can change her mind—get it done so you can breathe a sigh of relief. However, it's important to give yourself time and space to get to know her and to make this important decision. She's also going to need time to get to know you and make her decision as well. Make up a list of questions you want to ask a potential birth mother. You won't be able to ask her all of these questions the first time you talk, but it will be good to keep track of the questions to ask as you have further conversations. Remember that when you talk to a birth mother, you should always use the words "placing the child for adoption" instead of saying "giving the child up for adoption." It is a subtle difference, but an important one.

Questions to ask a potential birth mother

- ◩ Why are you placing this child for adoption?

- ◩ How far along are you?

- ◩ What is your due date?

- ◩ Who knows about your pregnancy?

- ◩ Who is the birth father? Is he aware of the pregnancy?

- ◩ Have you seen a doctor?

- ◩ Who is your doctor?

- Do you have any medical conditions?

- Do you want open adoption, and if so, what do you mean by that term?

- What are you looking for in the adoptive parents?

- Do you have a job? What do you do?

- Do you smoke, drink, or take any medication?

- Are you taking prenatal vitamins?

- What is your family medical history?

- What is your ethnic heritage?

- How old are you?

- What education do you have?

- Where do you live? Whom do you live with?

- Are you in a relationship?

- Do you have other children? Have any other children of yours been placed for adoption?

- Have you talked with a counselor or adoption agency about placement?

- What kind of support system do you have in place?

- Can you share photos of yourself and other family members?

- How long have you known about the pregnancy?

Contact With a Birth Mother

Once you are in touch with a possible birth mother, it can be tempting to want to spend a lot of time talking to her and working things out. However, when a birth mother calls you (she should always call you—you should never make the initial call), you need to tell her a little about yourself, find out a little about her (such as when her due date is, how her health is, and if the birth father is in the picture at all), and then have her call your attorney. Your attorney isn't able to call her, so you need to stress to her the importance of calling your attorney herself. She has to take all of these first steps so that it is clear she is not being coerced or persuaded into the adoption. Your attorney will then proceed from there and make arrangements for medical exams, counseling, and for necessary paperwork. You will have many more opportunities to speak with the birth mother before either of you makes a final decision about the adoption, however as soon as you begin medical exams and therapy appointments, there will be expenses, so you probably want to look before you leap here and have some level of certainty that this birth mother is the right one for you.

If you and the birth mother live in different states, you will need to hire attorneys to represent you in your home state and in hers. First, choose an attorney in your home state. He will be able to locate an attorney in the other state to assist with the case.

Payments

The issue of payments involved in adoptions is a tricky one. It's unrealistic to expect a birth mother to place her child for adoption without any kind of financial assistance. Not only does she have expenses from prenatal medical care and the birth itself, but she also loses time from work, and puts a lot of emotional energy into the pregnancy as well. However, laws about adoption payments were created to make sure that babies are not bought and sold. Most states try to find a happy medium that allows adoptive parents to handle most of the outright expenses, but does not permit other money to change hands.

In most states, adoptive parents are expected to pay for the birth mother's (and the baby's) medical expenses (this includes mental health counseling) during the course of her pregnancy). If the birth mother has health insurance (and many do not) the expenses will be lower, because her health insurance will cover much of her care. As an adoptive parent you would be responsible for any amounts not covered by her insurance, including copays. When the baby is born, she would either have coverage under your policy or you would pay those expenses out of pocket until you are able to place her on your policy. Check with your insurance company to find out what documentation is required.

In some states, the law allows the adoptive parents to pay the birth mother's living expenses (basics such as rent, utilities, food, and so on) during the last trimester of the pregnancy. Payments are usually permitted only if they are "usual and customary" in the state—in other words, you can only pay what other parents in the state normally are paying for. So, buying her a BMW probably would not be considered "usual and customary." Always check with your attorney before making *any* payments to the birth mother so that you are sure you are following your state's law exactly. Adoptive parents can also pay for the birth mother's attorney's fees if she employs an attorney. None of these payments are refundable if the birth mother chooses to keep the baby (except in Idaho, where they are reimbursable).

When you go to court to legally finalize your adoption, you will have to disclose to the court any payments you have made to the birth mother, so there is accountability. It is important to be sure your payments will be approved by a judge.

States that specifically allow payment of birth mother's living expenses:

- Arizona: must be court approved over $1,000.

- California: must be requested in writing by birth mother.

- Connecticut: includes maternity clothes.

- Florida

- Idaho: payments may be made up to six weeks after the birth, not to exceed $2,000 without court permission.

- Illinois

- Indiana: payments may be made up to six weeks after the birth, not to exceed $3,000.

- Iowa

- Kansas

- Louisiana: payments may be made up to 45 days after the birth.

- Michigan: payments may be made up to six weeks after the birth.

- Minnesota: payments may be made up to six weeks after the birth.

- Missouri

- Nevada

- New Hampshire: payments may be made up to six weeks after the birth

- New Jersey

- New Mexico: payments may be made up to six weeks after the birth

- North Carolina: payments may be made up to six weeks after the birth

- North Dakota: payments may be made up to six weeks after the birth

- Oregon

- South Carolina: payment may be made for a reasonable period of time

- Tennessee: payments may not be made 45 days prior to birth or surrender or 30 days after without court approval

- Utah

- Vermont

- Virginia

- Wisconsin: up to $1,000

Counseling

Counseling is an important part of any adoption and it is particularly important in a parent-initiated adoption because there is no agency to do any screening or psychological evaluation for you. You'll need to ask the birth mother to attend counseling if she is serious about placing her baby for adoption. An initial evaluation can reveal potential problems and unresolved emotions she has about the adoption. Ongoing counseling will help her deal with the natural feelings she will have as she goes through the pregnancy, delivery, and the adjustment period afterwards, as well as the legal process. Your attorney can assist the birth mother in locating a counselor experienced in adoption.

Counseling can also be helpful for adoptive parents. As you wait for your baby to be born, you too will face anxiety, doubt, and fear. You may have difficulty trusting the birth mother or face worries about her changing her mind. A counselor can help you work through the process and stay focused on the goal of adding a child to your family.

You and the birth mother may also want to attend a few sessions together to work out any problems in your relationship. Counseling can be a good place to iron out difficulties with an open adoption plan. The prospective parents handle all therapy costs.

Home Studies

A home study is required in every adoption, even a parent-initiated one. If you are not working with an agency, you will need to find a social worker who can prepare your home study. Your attorney should be able to recommend someone. If you're working with a facilitator, he or she should be able to provide a name as well.

You may wish to get your home study done before you begin an active search for a birth mother, so that you can tell any potential birth mothers that you've already completed that step of the process. Having a completed home study offers an extra measure of security to some birth mothers.

Your Relationship With the Birth Mother

Because you're making up the rules for the adoption as you go along, you can have as much or as little contact with the birth mother as you prefer, both during the pregnancy and after. Each adoption is different so you will have to work within your comfort zone, as well as that of the birth mother. Your attorney or adoption agency can be helpful intermediaries in this situation and can help establish and communicate some basic rules for contact. You really need to think about how close and involved you want to become. Some adoptive parents want to make the birth mother almost a member of their family and some invite her to come stay with them during the pregnancy. This can be good because it gives you a front row seat to the pregnancy and gives you more control over what she does, but it can also be bad because it can lead to personality conflicts.

In addition to your relationship during the pregnancy, you need to consider how you want to handle the birth. Some birth mothers and adoptive parents make arrangements for the adoptive parents to be present at the birth—which can mean you're in the delivery room or that you're waiting outside. You need to work this out with your birth mother in advance. If you are present at the hospital, make sure the staff is aware you are the adoptive parent so that you can have access to the birth mother and baby (the birth mother will need to give her specific consent for this because the baby legally belongs to her until the placement occurs). If you have a partner and live in a state where only one of you can adopt the child at a time, or where second parent adoptions are not permitted for same sex couples, there will be a disparity in the way the hospital personnel treat the parent who is adopting first and the parent who is adopting second (or not legally adopting at all) because only one of you will have an "in progress" link to the baby.

Other adoptive parents wait at home for the call that the baby has arrived. There is no right answer, and whatever works best in your situation is fine.

Finalization

As with any other adoption, the adoption is not finalized and complete until the legal waiting period is up. See Chapter 3—this varies with the state the child is born in. It is essential that you use an attorney to draft all the adoption documents. Be sure that the papers you and the birth mother sign and present to the court are correct for your state and legally acceptable to the court. The birth mother must have her own attorney and cannot use yours.

Once the waiting period concludes, the adoption is legalized and you become a parent. Parent-initiated adoptions are usually looked at more closely than agency adoptions by courts to be sure that state laws about payment and consent have been carefully followed, but your attorney will make sure that all the legal details are taken care of. For more information about adoption paperwork and about birth certificates, see Chapter 3.

Chapter 8

Foster Parenting

Foster care exists to provide a safe home (a real home, not an institution) for children whose parents have abused or neglected them, and also for some children who are juvenile delinquents. Some of these children are in foster care only temporarily—until their parents get their rights back (and two out of three children are back with their parents within a year). Others are freed for adoption, meaning their biological parents' legal ties to them are completely dissolved and they can be adopted, but until that happens, they live in foster care.

Foster care is overseen by the state, but individual foster homes are usually directly managed by private agencies. These agencies recruit, train, and monitor foster parents. To find foster care agencies in your area, contact your state foster care specialists.

There are never enough foster care parents. Many foster homes are overcrowded. There are over 500,000 children in foster homes in the United States, and while the number of children in foster homes is growing, the number of available foster homes is decreasing. This means more children are being placed in institutional care situations because there is simply no room for them in actual homes.

Requirements

To qualify as a foster parent, you must:

- ◪ Be 21 years of age or older.

- ◪ Have regular employment or a regular source of income (your or your partner).

- ◪ Have no felony record and pass a criminal record check.

- ◪ Complete a home assessment.

- ◪ Provide character references.

- ◪ Complete a foster-parent training course.

Most states have no restrictions on gay singles or couples becoming foster parents (although, some states have tried to pass such laws and Utah prohibits unmarried cohabiting couples from being foster parents). In fact, there is a perception in this area that gays and lesbians make good foster parents because they are already used to living lives that are seen as different from other people's. Many people have a very hard time understanding foster care, and foster parents often talk about how their friends are afraid to invite them and their foster children over or how people look at them strangely in stores with all their children along. So, to a certain extent, foster parents feel ostracized, which is a feeling that gays and lesbians already know how to cope with. To become a foster parent, you'll need to find an agency that works with gay foster parents and is not prejudiced.

You don't need to own a home, but you have to have room in your home for a foster child to be considered. Some states have restrictions on the ownership of firearms with foster children in the home, so be sure to ask about that if you own a firearm.

Foster care might be for you if:

- ◪ You are able to cope with change.

- ◪ You are interested in focusing your energies on children who might have troubled lives.

- ◪ You understand that foster children come from all different backgrounds and you are comfortable with that.

- ◪ You can work well with people in authority and are able to be a team player.

- ◪ You can accept the fact that you might have to send a child you love back to his or her family, even if you believe that family is toxic.

- ◪ You can create household rules and routines and apply them fairly.

- ◪ You aren't as concerned with having a child of your own, as much as you are concerned about improving the lives of children and offering a safe haven.

- ◪ You realize that you won't be able to adopt many of the children who come into your home.

- ◪ You're willing to be ready day or night, at a moment's notice, to take in a child.

- ◪ You're good at calming children in stressful situations, or think you might be good at it.

- ◪ You're willing to facilitate visits between the foster child and his parents, without getting embroiled in the conflict of the situation.

- ◪ You understand that your role is not to judge, but to provide open arms.

How to Apply

The first step towards becoming a foster parent is attending an orientation meeting. Contact your state foster care association, your local department of social services, or family and children for information on dates and times.

Nuts and Bolts of Foster Care

When a child is placed with you, you are responsible for the day-to-day care of the child. You make rules and make sure the child goes to school, eats well, is dressed properly, and behaves. You will have ongoing contact with the caseworker from the agency you are licensed through, as well as possibly the state caseworker. The caseworker is the one who has ultimate authority though, and you need permission for things such as taking the child out of town on vacation or obtaining long-term medical care for the child.

You will receive a monthly stipend that is meant to cover the child's expenses (but do not need to provide an accounting). This varies by state and by the age of the child, but is between $350 and $750 per month. You're not going to get rich being a foster parent, at least not in the monetary sense. You are responsible for buying the child's clothes, toys, school supplies, and food. If you work and you need daycare, you will be responsible for this expense as well. Most foster children receive Medicaid, which pays for their medical expenses.

Many foster homes accept several children. In most states, if you are going to take in boys and girls, they must have separate bedrooms and bathrooms. Foster children of the same sex can share a bedroom. When you become a foster parent you can choose to limit the ages and sexes of the children you want to take in. Teens, sibling groups, and teen mothers are the foster children that are the hardest to place.

About 30 percent of the children in foster care have severe emotional, behavioral, or developmental problems, so as a foster parent, you've got to be flexible and creative. You also need to be ready to seek out resources to help you with different problems. Foster parents spend a lot of time bringing children to doctor appointments and therapy appointments, and also need to connect with the child's school.

One important aspect of foster care is privacy. You're not allowed to discuss the details of the child's history, parents, or situation with anyone. A foster parent's role is to provide care for the child, with the goal of reuniting the family. Until a child is freed for adoption, the ultimate plan must be that the child will return to her parents.

For information about foster care, visit the National Foster Parent Association at *www.nfpainc.org* or go to The Dave Thomas Foundation for Adoption at *www.DaveThomasFoundationforAdoption.org*.

Family-to-Family Foster Care

Family-to-family foster care is a growing trend where foster parents take on responsibility not only for foster children, but also become involved with the children's parents on an ongoing and continuing basis. Taking the children away temporarily usually does not solve the problems in the home (it is after all, just a temporary fix), but if the parents themselves are mentored, assisted, and encouraged to be involved in their children's lives, they can improve their parenting skills and create a better home for their children. Involvement in this type of program requires even more dedication than regular fostering because you're not only taking on care of the children, but you're becoming immersed in the family's problems. It also requires more skills. For many people, parenting skills come naturally, but social work skills needed to work with adults who are in difficulty may not be as natural. The upside is that these programs can make a lasting difference and help children as well as parents. If you're interested in this type of program, inquire at your local department of families and children if there are any such programs in your area.

Foster Parent Rights

Foster parents have no automatic right to adopt a child who has been placed with them, and if the agency and the court determine it is in the child's best interests to be adopted by someone else, there's nothing you can do. Foster parents have no control or say over what happens to the children they raise unless they are able to adopt them.

When you're considering foster care, it is easy to paint a rosy picture for yourself of what it would be like. Because of this, it's a good idea to talk to some foster parents in your area to get a first-hand account of what it is like. The children who are placed in foster care are often removed from their homes abruptly and in the middle of a very stressful situation. The children are frightened, angry, resentful, and upset at the entire situation and often do not respond positively to the foster parents immediately. Imagine how you would feel if a stranger took you out of your bed in the middle of the night with nothing more than the clothes on your back and your parents were frantic and panicked? However, as hard as foster parenting can be, it has many, many rewards. Foster parents are able to show children love and kindness, which they may have never experienced before in their lives. There are many children who develop very close bonds with their foster parents that last the rest of their lives, whether they are reunited with their parents or not.

Find a list of state foster care specialists at *www.adopting.org/adoptions/foster-care-specialists-by-state.html.*

Find state foster care agencies at *http://foster.parenting.adoption.com/agencies/agencies.php.*

Chapter 9

Sperm Donors

Donated sperm allows lesbian singles or couples to have a family, with very little involvement by other people, such as adoption agencies, social workers, or fertility clinics. When you decide to start a family this way, you don't need to deal with home studies and waiting periods. If you use a sperm bank, you don't even need a lawyer. It is the simplest and fastest way to create a family and a child one partner is biologically related to. Some lesbians use people they know as sperm donors so they don't need to go use a sperm bank or clinic. Others choose to use sperm donor banks (which are often very lesbian-friendly these days and find a sperm donor that way).

Insemination

Insemination is the procedure in which sperm is inserted into a woman's body to attempt conception. Insemination can happen in a doctor's office or at home. Some women use intrauterine insemination, where the sperm is directly placed in the uterus in a doctor's office to increase their chances of becoming pregnant.

Note that when a woman who is married gives birth, the child is legally that of her spouse. Thus in states where gays were allowed to marry or obtain civil rights at the time this book was written, a married same-sex partner would be the child's legal parent. Hopefully, if more states recognize the right of same-sex couples to marry, this may become more common. Should your state adopt same-sex marriage, you get married, and consider insemination, you will need to find out if your state requires that a married partner consent to the insemination. Many states now require a husband in a heterosexual couple to consent to the insemination because the child is legally his (and he's thus responsible for child support).

> Read a booklet about insemination from The American Society of Reproductive Medicine at *www.asrm.org/Literature/patient.html*.

Known Sperm Donors

Many lesbian couples consider using a relative of the partner who will not be carrying the pregnancy, so that the child will be biologically related to both parents. Using a friend is another option for both singles and couples. The main advantage to a known donor is that you know exactly where the sperm came from and you know what the person's traits are, what his personality is like, what his medical history is, and you can have ongoing contact with him after the pregnancy so that the child can someday meet him in the future. He can also become a male role model and be involved in the child's life (not necessarily as a "dad" but perhaps a special uncle), which is important to some women. Another advantage of post-pregnancy contact is that you will have access to any medical information that comes to light after the insemination—for example if the donor is diagnosed with diabetes or heart disease.

The disadvantages of a known donor are the emotional complications that can ensue. If the donor is a family member or close friend, you could come to resent his presence in the child's life or the donor could come to feel resentful about his small role in the child's life. You might have different expectations about his role and connection to the child which only becomes evident as the child grows, no matter how closely you've tried to sort it out before the pregnancy. If you were friends, you risk the possibility of your friendship changing because of the insemination.

It is very important that, even though you know the donor, his sperm be tested for sexually transmitted diseases. Testing for HIV takes up to six months. Some women are willing to take the risk with a close family member or friend, but it's not recommended.

> For information on home insemination, visit:
> *http://homeinseminations.homestead.com/index.html* or
> *www.fertilityplus.org/faq/homeinsem.html.*

It is important that all the parties involved in the insemination procedure (the woman being inseminated, the donor, and the woman's partner, if any) obtain counseling. This will not only help the parties work through any problems they have with the procedure, but will also help ensure that problems will not appear in the future. Counseling ensures that everyone involved is certain about the decision and is emotionally able to handle its repercussions. Counseling also forces you to consider possible scenarios you might not consider, and helps you plan out solutions to them. Practically speaking, a lot of women who do home inseminations do not use counseling, but it is what the experts recommend.

Working out your relationship with a known donor can be an ongoing process, but it's important that you come to a meeting of the minds about his role and your ongoing relationship with him before you do an insemination. You want to have some basic parameters in place and make sure everyone has the same expectations. Many women and couples find that after the baby is born, and as she grows, they have to make some adjustments to what they thought would work. Some things just feel uncomfortable and sometimes people don't really understand what the emotional implications of things will be until they live them. The key is to for all of you to be honest with each other, now and in the future, and be committed to a plan that will offer your child a happy life.

Agreements With Known Donors

Even though you have some kind of relationship with the known donor, it is essential that you sign a legally binding insemination agreement. You cannot leave this up to trust. All of your rights and responsibilities to each other have to be spelled out. It is important that you use a reproductive law attorney to draft an agreement that will meet the requirements of your state. You may need to file court papers in which the donor formally gives up his rights to the child in order for the agreement to be legally binding in your state.

The agreement will have the donor give up all rights to custody or visitation with the child. This is essential so that he does not later change his mind and decide to seek custody.

The woman receiving the sperm gives up all rights to seek anything from the donor, including child support. If you have a partner, it is a good idea to have her sign the agreement as well.

FDA Regulations

The FDA now bans gay men from being anonymous sperm donors. The regulation is meant to provide protection against HIV, however many doctors are refusing to perform inseminations with known donors who are gay because of these rules. If you would like to use a known donor who is gay and your doctor refuses to use any gay donors, your donor will need to lie about his sexual identity, or you will need to use home insemination.

Unknown Donors

Unknown donors are generally located through a sperm bank. Sperm banks pay donors for their sperm and carefully screen donors and their sperm for medical conditions and disease. The sperm is frozen and preserved until testing is complete because it takes months for HIV testing to conclude. The sperm bank makes sure that donors and the women who receive the donations receive counseling to help them cope with the decision. The woman using the sperm is charged a small fee—often between $200 and $400 for the sperm, not including the cost of the insemination procedure. The woman receiving the sperm usually must also undergo medical testing herself—including HIV, syphilis, rubella, and so on.

Sperm banks offer profiles of donors that include medical history, physical attributes, mental abilities, personality traits, and photos of the donor as an adult or child. The bank may also offer video and audio tapes of the donor. Clients of the sperm bank can choose a donor that is physically similar to them or their partner in some way or who meets other criteria they have. You may be able to flip through books that list donors, or use a computer to help you locate donors that fit your preferences.

There is currently no federal government regulation of sperm banks in the United States, although four states do license sperm banks: California, Maryland, Massachusetts, and New York. Look for a sperm bank that is accredited by the American Association of Tissue Banks (*www.aatb.org*), but realize that most are not. Be certain that any bank you consider follows the guidelines recommended by the American Society of Reproductive Medicine (ASRM, *www.asrm.org*).

An important thing to discuss with a sperm bank is whether they monitor the number of offspring from each donor. If they don't, there's the possibility that your child could have a large number of half-siblings, increasing the chances that two might actually marry someday without realizing, which could lead to genetic problems for their children. You'll also want to make sure the sperm bank will allow you to reserve additional sperm for future use in case you want your child to have a brother or sister.

The following states require HIV screening of donor sperm used at sperm banks:

- Arizona

- California

- Connecticut

- Delaware

- Florida

- Idaho

- Illinois

- Indiana

- Iowa

- Kentucky

- Louisiana

- Maryland

- Michigan

- Montana

- North Carolina

- North Dakota

- Ohio

- Oklahoma

- Rhode Island

- Virginia

- West Virginia

- Wisconsin

You can find an extensive list of sperm banks online at *www.fertilityplus.org/faq/donor.html*.

The sperm bank has a written agreement with the donor and a separate agreement with you. You won't know the donor's name and he won't know yours. These contracts are set up to ensure that both you and the donor are protected from any future problems with custody or support. It's a good idea to have your contract reviewed by a reproductive rights attorney before signing it.

> *FamilyPride.org* has a list of sperm banks known to be
> lesbian-friendly on the FAQs in the education section
> of their Website.

The following states have laws that automatically remove
parental rights of donors donating to a sperm bank:

- ☑ Alabama

- ☑ California

- ☑ Colorado

- ☑ Connecticut

- ☑ Idaho

- ☑ Illinois

- ☑ Kansas

- ☑ Minnesota

- ☑ Missouri

- ☑ Montana

- ☑ Nevada

- ☑ New Hampshire

- ☑ New Jersey

- ☑ New Mexico

- ☑ North Dakota

- ☑ Ohio

- Oregon

- Texas

- Virginia

- Washington

- Wisconsin

- Wyoming

If you are ordering sperm from a sperm bank for home insemination, the sperm bank may require a physician's authorization to release it because donor sperm is considered a medical substance. Thus it is necessary to see a doctor and have her agree to or approve your plans for home insemination through a sperm bank. Some physicians will require you to come into the office for the insemination, but a growing number are amenable to home inseminations.

If you're interested in using sperm from gay men, there is a sperm bank that specializes, called Rainbow Flag Health Services, in San Francisco. Read more on their Website at *www.gayspermbank.com*.

When choosing a sperm bank, ask the following questions:

- How long have you been in business at this location?

- Are you licensed or accredited by any state or organization?

- Do you follow ASRM guidelines?

- What procedures are used to test the health of the donors and the sperm?

- What other screening do you with donors (such as mental health screening)?

- How long do you keep records? Do you follow ASRM record-keeping guidelines?

- Can clients select the donor themselves or do you make the selection?

- What donor information is available?

- Are current and baby pictures available for each donor?

- Are personal statements available from donors?

- What post-thaw sperm count do you require?

- Is the health of the donors monitored on an ongoing basis after donations are made?

- Do you track the number of pregnancies per donor? Is donor sperm available for a second child?

- Do you act as a middleman should the child, once she is grown, wish to contact the donor?

- Do you store cells from the donor that can later be tested if necessary?

- Is there a difference between the number of total donors and the actual number of donors available? (Some donors may not be available because of demand.)

Legal Parents

The woman who carries the pregnancy is the legal parent of the child. The sperm donor has no rights to the child and cannot be held liable for support. The woman's partner is not a legal parent, unless they live in Massachusetts or California, where courts have held that children born to one parent during a committed relationship is the legal child of the other parent. In Vermont there is a case currently working its way through the court system about whether a same-sex partner is automatically a legal parent of a child born to a partner during a civil union. At the time this book was written, there was no final decision yet.

In all other states, the partner will need to legally adopt the child after the birth using a second parent adoption process, if this is legal in your state described in Chapter 4). The mother will be the only legal parent of the child until this point.

Birth Certificates

When your child is born, in most states you can choose any last name you want for him, so you could use one partner's last name, a combination of both partner's names, or any other name you choose. Some partners choose one last name for the family, legally change the name of the partner with the other name, and then use that family name on the birth certificate. Although it is legal to choose any name, some clerks who handle the processing of birth certificates may not be aware of this, so you may need to do some arm-twisting. You can't list the partner who didn't carry the pregnancy as a parent on the birth certificate, except in California or Massachusetts.

Protecting Your Family

If you live in a state where your partner cannot adopt the child born to you by insemination, you will need to take steps such as a will and school and medical consents to make sure her role in your child's life is protected. Something else some lesbians have done is to each carry a child using the same sperm donor. This means their children are biological siblings, and should something happen to one of the women, a court would not separate the children, meaning the remaining partner would most likely be given custody of the child she is not biologically related to.

Some women have wondered if using an egg from one partner and having the other partner carry the pregnancy would offer them protection, because in all states, if a woman gives birth to a child, she is the legal parent even if she does not have a biological connection to the child. The problem is that you must have help with egg retrieval and clinics that do egg retrieval, fertilization, and implantation require that the woman providing the egg sign away her rights—she must be an egg donor. In theory, it is possible to use one partner's egg and have the other carry the pregnancy, but it would be difficult to find a clinic willing to do so. However, a California court decision held that when a child is born to a lesbian partner, the other partner is also a legal parent. That was actually based on one case in which one partner did donate her egg to the other. The court held that even though the donor signed away her rights as a donor, she could not truly do so in this situation.

Fertility Problems

For many women, insemination works, but for others, they have a difficult time getting pregnant. If you're trying and getting nowhere, first consider handing the process over to a physician. Home insemination is wonderful, but a physician may have more experience and better odds. Your OB/GYN can also talk to you about how to accurately use basal body temperature to predict ovulation, as well as ovulation predictor kits. If you're not ovulating, your physician can prescribe a drug to kick start that process for you.

If simple insemination does not work, you may need to move up to intrauterine insemination, described earlier in this chapter. If that is not successful, you should consider seeing a reproductive endocrinologist and having a complete fertility work up done. If you're using a sperm bank, they should have analyzed the sperm to make sure it is fertile and active, but you may need some help with your own reproductive system.

Finding Medical Professionals You Are Comfortable With

If you need medical help to conceive, the most important thing you can do is select doctors and clinics that you are comfortable with. If you are working with providers who are not sensitive to your needs, or whom you just feel uncomfortable with, the entire process will be more difficult for you.

The first place to start is with your OB/GYN. Presumably you trust him or her, so ask for a referral to a specialist. If you like your OB/GYN, then hopefully he will refer you to a specialist you will prefer. If you aren't happy with that referral, ask for another. If there is a medical school in your area, call them and ask if the school is involved in a fertility clinic in your area. Talk to other women or couples you know who have used assisted reproduction about doctors and facilities.

Before visiting a specialist or clinic, call and ask if the providers on staff are board certified or board eligible in reproductive endocrinology. Fertility specialists should be certified in both of these areas. If the clinic has an I-vetro Fertilization lab, ask if it is accredited by the College of American Pathologists. All labs of any kind must be accredited under the federal Clinical Laboratory Improvement Amendment (CLIA). Ask if the physicians are members of the American Society of Reproductive Medicine. Most reputable clinics also have the following specialists on staff: reproductive immunologist, embryologist, reproductive urologist, andrologist, and genetic counselors.

> You can check accreditation at:
> The American College of Obstetricians and Gynecologists at *www.acog.org*.
> The College of American Pathologists at *www.cap.org*.
> American Board of Medical Specialties at *www.abms.org*.
> American Society of Reproductive Medicine *at www.asrm.org*.

Questions to ask a fertility specialist:

- Where did you go to medical school and complete your residency?

- How many years have you been a fertility specialist?

- How many reproductive endocrinologists are on staff?

- Will we work with one doctor or several?

- Is there someone on call after hours?

- Are you affiliated with a hospital?

- What insurance plans do you accept?

- Are payment plans an option?

- How much will the proposed treatment cost? What does that include?

- What is your practice's number of take-home babies?

- What treatments and services do you offer?

- Can you provide referrals should we require other treatments?

- Have you worked with lesbians before?

> Get support and information about infertility issues from Resolve, The National Infertility Association at (888) 623-0744, or *www.resolve.org*.

Your Right to ART

Fertility clinics cannot turn you away because of a disability or discriminate against you because of your race or ethnic background. Unfortunately, there is no law that prohibits discrimination by fertility clinics because of sexual orientation. At the time this book was written, a California case, *North Coast Women's Care Medical Group, Inc. v. Superior Court* (Benitez), in which a lesbian was discriminated against by a clinic, was currently making its way through the court system. If you are worried about discrimination, call ahead and specifically ask if they have worked with lesbians before.

Initial Visit

When you visit a fertility specialist, it is important to bring medical records, test results, and reports with you. Both partners should be at the first visit so that both can meet the doctors.

Ask yourselves if you feel comfortable with the people you meet there and with the general atmosphere. Are you able to be open about your relationship if you came with your partner? You also need to be truthful with yourselves about what you can afford. Try to get clear answers about success rates and evaluate what you are told with a critical eye.

Setting Limits

Most women enter the world of assisted reproduction slowly—first with fertility drugs and then gradually moving on to other procedures. When you first begin to work with medical assistance to get pregnant or have a child, it's important to either think through on your own or have a frank discussion with your partner about what types of medical assistance you are comfortable with. Once you begin to work with fertility specialists, a whole world of possibilities opens before you.

Realize that what you think you know about your feelings and preferences now may change. If you move through different procedures with no success, you may feel that the desire to have a child is more urgent than any objections you might have had earlier to certain types of fertility assistance.

Privacy

You will also have to make some choices about who you will tell about your insemination procedures and what information you are willing to share with family, friends, and so on. You're not obligated to tell anyone of course, but most single women and couples find they need the support that friends and family can provide.

Because insemination in a doctor's office is a medical procedure, it is protected by HIPAA, the Health Insurance Portability and Accountability Act. All of your records are confidential and cannot be shared without your permission.

Affording Insemination and Fertility Treatments

Many states only provide coverage of insemination or fertility treatments if the woman is using her husband's sperm (visit *www.asrm.org* for up-to-date state insurance coverage laws), or if she has been trying to conceive and has not been successful. Just because your state does not require coverage though does not mean you won't have it. Check with your insurance company before beginning any treatments to find out exactly what is covered and what conditions must be met. For example, some require that in order to receive coverage for fertility treatments, a woman must have tried for at least six months to become pregnant. Ask about copays and costs that are not covered.

You should also find out if your employer offers Flexible Spending Accounts (FSAs), which allow you to have money taken out of your paycheck pretax. You can use this to pay for medical expenses.

> Details about expenses that FSAs can be used for are available at *www.irs.goc/publications/p502/index.html.* You can find out more information on state insurance requirements for infertility treatments are available a*www.fertilityjourney.com.*

It is also possible to get financing for fertility treatments. Many clinics work with finance companies that offer interest rates that are lower than you could obtain on your own. Be sure to get complete details on any financing arrangement though and avoid any with balloon payments.

If you incur large fertility costs, you may be able to deduct them on your federal income taxes, if your expenses exceed 7.5 percent of your gross income.

Chapter 10

Using a
Surrogate

Surrogacy allows a gay man to be biologically related to his child. The man provides sperm and the surrogate is a woman who agrees to carry a pregnancy for him, or for him and his partner. There are two types of surrogacy. In traditional surrogacy, the surrogate's own eggs are used and are inseminated with the intended father's sperm. If a gay couple is having the child, some choose to mix their sperm and not know for certain whose sperm impregnated the egg. Gestational surrogacy occurs when the surrogate is implanted with an embryo created with the intended father's sperm and a donor egg (not the surrogate's own egg, so she is not genetically related to the child). If a couple is having the child, it would be possible to use a donor egg obtained from a family member of the parent who is not donating the sperm, so that the baby could be biologically related to both partners.

Surrogacy can cost from $25,000 to more than $50,000 depending on the difficulty involved with conception, the medical issues present in the pregnancy, and what expenses and costs the intended parents are responsible for under the contract.

Surrogacy Laws

There is no general legal trend about surrogacy in the United States yet and states tend to be all over the board. There are five general categories of states:

States where it is a crime to pay for surrogacy:

- Michigan

- New Mexico

- New York

- Washington

States where surrogacy contracts are unenforceable (this means you can't ask a court to enforce it, however you are free to enter into one, knowing that you will not be able to obtain assistance from the court):

- District of Columbia

- Indiana

- Louisiana

- Nebraska

- New York

- North Dakota

States which recognize surrogacy agreements through laws:

- Arkansas

- Florida: reasonable compensation is permitted.

- Illinois: procedure is relatively simple

- New Hampshire: The intended parent is listed on the first birth certificate but it is not issued for 72 hours after the birth.

- Nevada

- Tennessee

- Texas

- Utah: Only infertile heterosexual married couples may enter into a surrogacy agreement. Surrogates must be financially stable—not on welfare—and must have previously carried and delivered a baby. Surrogacy is not permitted where the embryo is completely donated (not related to either intended parent).

- Washington: Only unpaid surrogacy is allowed.

- Virginia: has a prebirth procedure and allows the intended parent to be listed on the first birth certificate.

States with case law about surrogacy:

- California: permits surrogacy

- Massachusetts: A recent case encouraged the legislature to enact laws permitting surrogacy.

- Ohio: Has case law pertaining to heterosexual intended parent couples

- Oklahoma: permit surrogacy but requires the surrogate's husband (if any) to refuse to consent to what it is technically considered an egg donation to her (so that he has no legal obligation to the child)

- Kentucky: Prohibits surrogacy programs and payments, but this is largely unenforced.

All other states fall into the category of states that do not address surrogacy in any way.

Surrogacy Legal Process

In states that do not have laws stating otherwise, when a woman gives birth to a child, she is the legal mother of the child, even if she is not the biological mother of the child or has entered into a surrogacy contract. If the woman is married, her husband is considered to be the child's legal father until it is proven otherwise.

When a surrogacy agreement is entered into, the surrogate's husband must be a party to the contract and must revoke his rights to the child. The intended father, if he is the biological father, can then obtain an order of paternity. In some states this can happen during the pregnancy. This then gives him the legal right to have access to the child at the hospital and to take the child home without any additional legal steps. If the father has a partner, he must adopt the child using a second parent adoption procedure (see Chapter 3).

California Procedure

California is the only state that has a well-established procedure for legalizing surrogate births, and because of this, California has really become the surrogacy capital of the United States. Many people go to California to find surrogates and enter into surrogacy contracts in that state because the laws are so clear and welcoming. Once the surrogate is pregnant, the intended parents first file a court case. The surrogate and her husband consent to the surrogacy in the court. The court then issues a judgment that the intended parent or parents are the legal parents. The intended parents then can inform the hospital of this and the birth certificate will be issued to them, and they have the right to select the child's name. All the legal steps are taken care of before the baby is even born, which can ease a lot of worries.

However, if the surrogate provides the egg, she cannot relinquish her rights until the child is born (as in an adoption proceeding). In this case, the intended father can bring a paternity case during the pregnancy. The surrogate and her husband consent and he is the legal father, but the ruling cannot be finalized until after the birth. If the father has a partner, he must use the second parent adoption procedure to legalize his role.

Illinois Procedure

Illinois passed the Gestational Surrogacy Law in 2005 that permits intended parents to have their rights recognized before the birth of the child (similar to California). There must be a contract for the surrogacy and a statement by a physician of the intended parent's inability to have children. The surrogate must already have given birth to one child, be at least 21 years old, have undergone counseling, and obtained the advice of an attorney. The medical procedure must be performed in Illinois.

Surrogacy Programs

Many men locate a surrogate through a surrogacy program run through a fertility clinic. The program handles the matching of parents and surrogates as well as the medical procedures.

Adoption agencies also often run surrogacy programs. These programs locate potential surrogates, prescreen them, and match them with parents, and then the actual medical part of the surrogacy is carried out at a fertility clinic. Adoption agencies that have surrogacy programs treat the entire process in the same way they would a regular adoption and require home studies, counseling, and communication between the parties.

When choosing a surrogacy program, ask the following questions:

- ◪ How do you recruit and locate surrogates?

- ◪ How do you screen potential surrogates?

- ◪ How do you screen the intended parents?

- ◪ Do you work with the intended gay parents?

- ◪ Do you provide counseling for both surrogates and intended parents?

- ◪ What is your role in coordinating the surrogacy?

- ◪ What fees are involved?

- ◪ Are the fees refundable if the surrogacy is not completed? Does this differ with miscarriage, as opposed to a surrogate who changes her mind?

- ◪ Is there a waiting list?

- How many potential surrogates do you have in the program?

- How many intended parents are you working with now? How many are openly gay?

- Will you work with surrogates brought in by the intended parents?

- What kind of relationship do you recommend that intended parents have with their surrogate?

- Is there any post-birth contact with your program?

- Have any of your surrogates changed their minds after becoming pregnant? How do you handle this situation?

- How many births does your program have a year? How many total births have you had? What percent result in successful placement?

- How long have you been doing this?

- Can you provide the names of parents to contact for references?

- Do intended parents have the right to refuse proposed surrogates?

- Does the surrogate have her own attorney when signing the agreement?

- What kind of background information do you provide about the surrogate?

- How do you deal with the surrogate's expenses? How are they accounted and paid for?

It's important to choose a surrogacy program you feel comfortable with and confident in. Once you find a potential surrogate, she needs to undergo physical and mental exams before you go any further in the process. The surrogate will also want to get to know you and decide if she feels comfortable with you—you of course will do the same thing with her. Because surrogacy involves a large degree of trust, it's important to use a surrogate that you are completely comfortable with. The ideal surrogate is married and has children of her own. She understands what pregnancy and birth are like and also knows the kinds of feelings to expect after the baby is born.

> The largest and most well-known surrogacy agency that serves the gay community is Growing Generations (*www.growinggenerations.com*).

Finding a Surrogate on Your Own

Another option for surrogacy is to locate a surrogate on your own, without using a program. A relative of your partner or a close friend may be willing to be a surrogate. Of course, in this situation, it is essential to use a reproductive law attorney who will advise you about the laws in your state and who will draw up the contract. The agreement is going to be key because you want to be sure the surrogate gives up all of her rights to the child.

Everyone involved in the surrogacy process must obtain counseling (both before and during the pregnancy) because this emotional situation can be made even more complicated when you are using a surrogate you know and have an existing relationship with. It is possible to locate a stranger surrogate on your own, but this is not recommended because you can't perform the same sophisticated screening and psychological evaluation that an agency or clinic can.

Surrogacy Agreements

The most important feature of a surrogacy agreement is that it revokes all rights and responsibilities the surrogate and her husband have to the child. The intended parent or parents are the only legal parents to the child. Other important clauses include the following:

- The surrogate agrees to follow all medical advice, but medical decisions during the pregnancy are ultimately left up to her (she remains in control of her own body).

- The surrogate agrees to consider selective reduction (reducing the number of embryos that implant to prevent multiple birth) if necessary.

- The state where the child will be born is specified.

- The intended parents take on all financial and medical responsibility for the child.

- The intended parents have the right to name the child.

- The surrogate agrees to use her own medical insurance if she has any to cover her care during the pregnancy and delivery.

- The surrogate agrees to abstain from intercourse for a period of time while conception is attempted, to ensure that the intended father actually is the father.

It is essential that you use an attorney experienced in surrogacy agreements. Even if you are working with an agency or surrogacy program, you need to hire your own attorney to review the contract.

Some people may wonder why an agreement is so essential, particularly if they live in a state where the courts will not uphold a surrogacy agreement. Even if your courts will not enforce a surrogacy agreement, a contract is still important evidence should you get into a custody battle with your surrogate (rare, but still something you need to take precautions about). In addition, the negotiation process can help you spot problems and work out things that might become potential problems down the line. The agreement will spell out in clear terms what everyone is going to do and how all the issues involved will be handled. Also, when people sign their name to a contract they will usually feel obligated to carry out what they are agreeing to, so the agreement is an important way for both you and the surrogate to commit to the surrogacy. The negotiation process is also important because it's a time when you and the surrogate consider different scenarios and problems and can work them out in advance.

Read sample surrogacy contracts online at: *www.surrogacy.com/legals/gestcontract.html,* *www.surromomsonline.com/articles/contract.htm,* or *www.everythingsurrogacy.com/cgi-bin/main.cgi?test.*

Payment

The issue of paying surrogates is probably the most controversial part of the entire surrogacy process. Some people argue that paying a surrogate is the same as buying a baby and should be outlawed. Others feel that surrogates should be compensated for their time, physical discomfort, emotional turmoil, and extreme generosity. Because it is the only way a gay man can have a biological child, the legal protection of surrogacy should be an important issue for the gay community.

The intended parent is responsible for all medical expenses for the conception, pregnancy, and birth, except for those expenses covered by the surrogate's health insurance. In many cases, you will also be permitted to reimburse the surrogate for travel expenses, maternity clothes, lost wages, and additional childcare expenses (for her other children, or for times when she is going on appointments for the surrogacy). The laws governing this are the same as the laws governing reimbursement of expenses for a birth mother in an adoption.

Although these kinds of living expense payments are not permitted in some states, it is often possible to give the surrogate a gift. Discuss this option with your attorney to find out what is permissible in your state. If you violate the law about payments, your parent-child relationship is not jeopardized, however you may be subject to criminal penalties, so you want to make sure you are within the letter of the law on this.

Insurance Coverage

If your surrogate has insurance coverage, it should cover her pregnancy. Some surrogates do not wish to use their own insurance, although others are willing to do so if the intended parent pays all deductibles and copays. This is an important part of your agreement and should be included in your contract.

If your surrogate does not have health insurance coverage or will not be using her own coverage, you will need to pay for her medical expenses yourself, or help her obtain a health insurance policy, which may mean paying for it yourself. Your insurance will not provide coverage until the birth, and after that only if one parent is already a legal parent or if the child is officially placed with you as part of the adoption process.

Problems With Surrogacy

Many people are leery of surrogacy agreements, having heard about high-profile cases where surrogates changed their minds and refused to place the child with the intended parents. In some ways, the prospect of this is scarier than that of an adoption in which the birth mother changes her mind, because the intended father is also the biological and legal father of the baby.

The case law that exists about surrogacy concerns almost entirely heterosexual couples as the intended parents, however it's likely that the same standards would be applied to cases involving gay intended parents. The most famous case about surrogacy is the 1988 "Baby M" case from New Jersey. In that case, the court invalidated the surrogacy agreement but placed the baby with the biological father. The intended mother was not permitted to adopt because the surrogate (who was the biological mother) did not give her consent. The court found that the agreement was invalid because the surrogate was paid and said that if the agreement did not include payment, it would have been valid. So the worst case scenario is that if there is a problem, at the very least, the biological father will have custody of the child, but his partner may not be permitted to adopt, even if same sex second parent adoption is permitted in that state.

Another landmark case is the 1993 *Johnson v. Calvert* case from California. The surrogate was implanted with a zygote that was created using genetic material from both the intended mother and intended father. The surrogate was not biologically related to the child (the comparison for gay couples here would be if a zygote, or embryo, was created from the sperm of one of the partners and an egg from a relative of the other partner). The court held that the legal parents are those who were intended to be the parents under the agreement. According to the court, the parent of a surrogate is whoever is intended by the parties to be the parent, and not who is biologically related to the child or carries the pregnancy.

A 1994 Ohio case, *Belsito v. Clark*, held that unless a legal waiver or consent is provided, the people who provide the genetic material for the child are the natural parents of the child, meaning that if the surrogate provides the egg, she is the legal mother, but can give her consent for the adoption.

So, what happens if you use a surrogate and she changes her mind? In most cases, this doesn't happen, which is why it is important to use a respected surrogacy program that will carefully screen all potential surrogates and help you find a good match.

However, should something go wrong and the surrogate changes her mind, you first need to consult a reproductive rights attorney so that you can fully understand the laws in your state. As described earlier in this chapter, some states will not enforce surrogacy contracts, meaning that although you are free to enter into one, the court will not uphold it and enforce it if there are problems, and will instead apply state family laws about paternity and custody (it is for this reason that many couples carefully select the state in which the agreement is made and the child will be born).

If the intended father is the biological father of the child, he at the very minimum will have access to the child until the case is resolved. There will be a very good chance that the father will be able to obtain custody. If the surrogate provided the egg, she will at the very least be entitled to contact with the child (unless the birth is in a state where surrogacy contracts are enforced). If the surrogate did not provide the egg, the case for the intended parents is stronger, but not completely decisive, unless your state enforces surrogacy agreements.

Other Steps to Protect Yourself

As soon as you have entered into a surrogacy agreement, it is essential that the man providing the sperm (who will be the legal parent at birth) have a will drawn up, or update an existing will. You need to name a guardian for your child—if you have a partner, this is the only way you can hope that he will be given custody of the child should you pass away.

If you must go through a second parent adoption process to make your partner a legal parent, there will likely be weeks or months until the adoption is final. In this time period, you will have all the legal rights to make medical decisions for the child, but your partner will only have these rights if they are given to him in writing. See Chapter 12 for information about creating a written consent.

On the following two pages, you will see a sample of a California surrogacy form used in the adoption and surrogacy process.

FL-200

ATTORNEY OR PARTY WITHOUT ATTORNEY *(Name, state bar number, and address):*	To keep other people from seeing what you entered on your form, please press the Clear This Form button at the end of the form when finished.
TELEPHONE NO. *(Optional):* FAX NO. *(Optional):*	
E-MAIL ADDRESS *(Optional):*	
ATTORNEY FOR *(Name):*	

SUPERIOR COURT OF CALIFORNIA, COUNTY OF
STREET ADDRESS:
MAILING ADDRESS:
CITY AND ZIP CODE:
BRANCH NAME:

PETITIONER:

RESPONDENT:

PETITION TO ESTABLISH PARENTAL RELATIONSHIP ☐ Child Support ☐ Child Custody ☐ Visitation ☐ Other *(specify):*	CASE NUMBER:

1. Petitioner is
   a. ☐ the mother.
   b. ☐ the father.
   c. ☐ the child or the child's personal representative *(specify court and date of appointment):*
   d. ☐ other *(specify):*

2. The children are
   a. Child's name   Date of birth   Age   Sex

   b. ☐ a child who is not yet born.

3. The court has jurisdiction over the respondent because the respondent
   a. ☐ resides in this state.
   b. ☐ had sexual intercourse in this state, which resulted in conception of the children listed in item 2.
   c. ☐ other *(specify):*

4. The action is brought in this county because *(you must check one or more to file in this county):*
   a. ☐ the child resides or is found in the county.
   b. ☐ a parent is deceased and proceedings for administration of the estate have been or could be started in this county.

5. Petitioner claims *(check all that apply):*
   a. ☐ respondent is the child's mother.
   b. ☐ respondent is the child's father.
   c. ☐ parentage has been established by Voluntary Declaration of Paternity *(attach copy).*
   d. ☐ respondent who is child's parent has failed to support the child.
   e. ☐ *(name):*   has furnished or is furnishing the following reasonable expenses
      of pregnancy and birth for which the respondent as parent of the child is obligated:
      Amount   Payable to   For *(specify):*

   f. ☐ public assistance is being provided to the child.
   g. ☐ other *(specify):*

6. A completed *Declaration Under Uniform Child Custody Jurisdiction and Enforcement Act (UCCJEA))* (form FL-105) is attached.

Form Approved for Optional Use
Judicial Council of California
FL-200 [Rev. January 1, 2003]

PETITION TO ESTABLISH PARENTAL RELATIONSHIP
(Uniform Parentage)

Family Code, § 7630
www.courtinfo.ca.gov

American LegalNet, Inc.
www.USCourtForms.com

PETITIONER:	CASE NUMBER:
RESPONDENT:	

Petitioner requests the court to make the determinations indicated below.

7. PARENT-CHILD RELATIONSHIP
a. ☐ Respondent   b. ☐ Petitioner
c. ☐ Other (specify):   is the parent of the children listed in item 2.

8. CHILD CUSTODY AND VISITATION   Petitioner   Respondent   Joint   Other
a. Legal custody of children to   ☐   ☐   ☐   ☐
b. Physical custody of children to   ☐   ☐   ☐   ☐
c. Visitation of children:
     (1) ☐ None
     (2) ☐ Reasonable visitation.
     (3) ☐ Petitioner   ☐ Respondent   should have the right to visit the children as follows:

     (4) ☐ Visitation with the following restrictions (specify):

d. Facts in support of the requested custody and visitation orders are (specify):
     ☐ Contained in the attached declaration.
e. ☐ I request mediation to work out a parenting plan.

9. REASONABLE EXPENSES OF PREGNANCY AND BIRTH:
Reasonable expenses of pregnancy   Petitioner   Respondent   Joint
and birth be paid by   ☐   ☐   ☐
as follows:

10. FEES AND COSTS OF LITIGATION   Petitioner   Respondent   Joint
a. Attorney fees to be paid by   ☐   ☐   ☐
b. Expert fees, guardian ad litem fees, and other costs
of the action or pretrial proceedings to be paid by   ☐   ☐   ☐

11. NAME CHANGE
☐ Children's names be changed, according to Family Code section 7638, as follows (specify):

12. CHILD SUPPORT
The court may make orders for support of the children and issue an earnings assignment without further notice to either party.

13. I have read the restraining order on the back of the Summons (FL-210) and I understand it applies to me when this Petition is filed.

I declare under penalty of perjury under the laws of the State of California that the foregoing is true and correct.

Date:

▶

_____   _____
(TYPE OR PRINT NAME)   (SIGNATURE OF PETITIONER)

A blank Response to Petition to Establish Parental Relationship (form FL-220) must be served on the Respondent with this Petition.

> **NOTICE:** If you have a child from this relationship, the court is required to order child support based upon the income of both parents. Support normally continues until the child is 18. You should supply the court with information about your finances. Otherwise, the child support order will be based upon information supplied by the other parent.
> Any party required to pay child support must pay interest on overdue amounts at the "legal" rate, which is currently 10 percent.

FL-260 [Rev. January 1, 2003]   **PETITION TO ESTABLISH PARENTAL RELATIONSHIP**   Page 2 of 2

Print This Form	For your protection and privacy, please press the Clear This Form button after you have printed the form.	Clear This Form

Chapter 11

Other Parenting Options

There are some other options outside adoption and traditional insemination or surrogacy. Many are emerging technologies that have not been fully developed, but it is important to be aware of the other possible options that may soon be available.

Coparenting

In addition to insemination and surrogacy, there is a hybrid of the two, in which a lesbian woman and a gay man choose to have a child together. Each is a legal and biological parent of the child that is born. In some families, each parent lives in his own home and splits time with the child. In other families, they share one home. One or both may have partners who assume parental or stepparent roles.

If this is something you're considering, it is important to sit down and really hash out the details of how you will parent together. Think about how you will share your time with your child, how you will share expenses, and what you will do should you have a disagreement. If neither of you are partnered right now, consider how you will handle things should one of you become partnered. You'll also need to decide if you prefer home insemination or would like help from a doctor. See Chapter 9 for more information about insemination.

After your child is born, you should file a settlement agreement with your local family court that will legally lay out your parenting agreement and will provide that both of you have access to the child's medical and school records. If you don't have custody papers, you could have difficulty when your child starts school. Schools ask which parent the child lives with and often ask to see copies of custody papers. Having papers will also legally protect both of you. You are not required to file child support papers, unless that is part of what you've agreed to and you would like something formal and enforceable from a court.

Preserving Eggs and Sperm

Cryopreservation, sub-zero freezing of human cells, is used to freeze sperm, eggs, ovaries, and embryos and save them for future use by the person or couple who created them, or to save them for donation to other infertile singles or couples. Cryopreservation is an important option for those facing chemotherapy, which can permanently damage sperm and egg production capabilities, or for women who are approaching menopause and may not be able to produce viable eggs in the future. There is usually an up-front fee for cryopreservation (ranging up to $1,000) and then a monthly storage fee. Make sure the tissue bank you consider is a member of the American Association of Tissue Banks (*www.aatb.org*) and is accredited.

If you are transgender and plan to undergo gender-altering surgery, you may wish to consider freezing your sperm or eggs beforehand, in order to give yourself the option of one day parenting a child who is biologically related to you.

Embryo Donation

Embryo donation occurs when an egg that has been fertilized and has begun to develop into a baby (sometimes also called a zygote—but, technically an embryo is a few days older than a zygote) is donated to someone else who would parent the child. There are currently no known donations to gay singles or couples.

These embryos or zygotes are usually extras that have resulted when other couples have undergone ART procedures. Because these procedures usually produce more zygotes than are safe to implant at once, couples undergoing these procedures often freeze the extras. The original intent may be to save them for later ART cycles if the current one is unsuccessful. The couple may also intend to save them in order to have siblings later, but eventually decide they don't want to have any more children and the embryos are donated.

> Get more information on embryo donation from Reprotech at *www.reprot.com*, or The National Embryo Donation Center at *www.embryodonation.org*.

Although there are many couples producing many extra zygotes, few actually donate them to other couples. However, there have been at least 53 children born using embryo donation according to a recent survey by the Embryo Donation Task Force.

You don't have as much choice with embryo donations because there simply are not many donated and matching is done by the clinic, so you have little say. Another option is an embryo adoption. An outside agency that is not associated with the clinic handles the matching process. Recipients are provided with more information about the donors, and counseling and home studies are performed just as they would be in a traditional adoption. Donors have some say in choosing the recipient and also have the option of staying in touch with them and possibly knowing their genetic children at some point down the line.

A lesbian could carry a donated embryo and she would be the child's legal parent. Her partner could do a same-sex adoption. A gay man or couple could use a surrogate to carry a donated embryo and the process would be the same as a gestational surrogacy.

Generally two separate agreements are involved in embryo donation. The donors sign an agreement giving up all rights to the frozen embryos. This could occur years before a recipient is found. Often this is part of the original contract that the couple signs when they begin fertility treatments at the clinic. Most agreements specify what will happen to unused or extra embryos. The recipient signs a separate agreement with the clinic agreeing to accept the embryo and dealing with the medical risk factors involved. Donors and recipients usually have no direct contact and are not aware of each other's identity. Be sure to have your reproductive law attorney read any contract from a clinic before you sign it.

If you are interested in an embryo donation in which the donors are involved in the selection process you will find that there are no laws governing this process. Most agencies treat the process as a traditional adoption and have the donor and recipient sign consent forms as they would in a regular adoption. Note that there are no known gays or lesbians who have used this process, so it is uncharted territory as far as how gay-friendly the agencies are.

Embryo donation costs average $3,000 per transfer, plus any shipping costs.

Nuclear Transfer

Nuclear transfer is a process in which the nucleus of an egg cell, the part that contains the genetic material, is removed and replaced with another nucleus. This procedure could be used by women who are unable to produce viable egg cells on their own. The intended parent's genetic material would be implanted into an egg donated by another woman. The egg would then carry the intended parent's genes, but would also contain mitochrondrial genes from the donor. These genes do not determine physical traits but can carry inherited diseases, so the resulting child would be influenced by the donor but would be directly related to the intended mother. This newly formed egg could then be inseminated and placed in the intended mother's uterus, or in that of a surrogate. The procedure has been attempted with human eggs, but there have been no reported positive results at the time this book was written.

Another option with this technique would be to replace the nucleus of the donor egg with the nucleus from a sperm. The newly created egg could then be fertilized by a different sperm. A child born by this technique would have two genetic parents who are both male. Although this has not been attempted yet, it is something that would allow two gay men to have a child together, made up of their unique genetic material.

If this procedure should become available, complete consent of all the parties involved would be important (including the woman who provides the donor egg). A complete medical history is essential because the donor egg can carry disease even after the nucleus is removed. Additionally, the contract would completely revoke the donor's rights and responsibilities towards the egg and any resulting child. This procedure is currently banned in California under its human cloning law.

Cloning

Cloning has come to have quite a stigma associated with it. The type of cloning used in reproduction is called somatic nuclear cloning and is the same type that was used to create Dolly the sheep.

There are numerous applications of cloning that are useful and too often they are obscured by the emotional reaction people have to the word "cloning." Most people think of cloning as the process by which an exact replica of a specific human is created. In this technique, the nucleus of a cell is removed and is replaced with DNA from an adult. The result is an exact genetic twin to the person who donated the DNA.

Other applications may prove more useful and less controversial. Both sperm and eggs can be cloned, so a woman using assisted reproduction could go through just one egg harvesting cycle, clone the harvested eggs, and then have innumerable eggs available for future fertilization, avoiding the need to go through superovulation and the discomfort of the egg harvesting procedure again. Additionally if a man has low-sperm count, his sperm could be cloned, offering many more opportunities to create a baby.

Another type of cloning is embryo cloning. A lesbian couple using fertility treatments, or a gay man using surrogacy, could create just one successfully fertilized embryo and clone it so numerous attempts at implantation could be made.

Clonaid, a human cloning company, has reported the birth of five babies through the use of cloning. For more information about this company, see *www.clonaid.com,* or The Human Clone Rights Foundation at *www.humanclonerights.org.*

Clonaid is run by a religious cult called the Raelians. If you want more information or news reports about this group, do an Internet search using their name. The group is controversial and they have not yet provided any proof of their cloning claims.

Currently only a few states have created legislation banning reproductive cloning: Arkansas, California, Iowa, Michigan, North Dakota, Rhode Island, and Virginia.

If cloning should ever be an available choice, you should then review the results of studies that have been conducted and all the long-term data available. The laboratory and facilities performing the procedure should be experienced and have past successes with the treatment—the number of take-home babies per procedures performed.

There are few legal ramifications to cloning egg or sperm cells, if they are used for one's own use. If cells such as these are cloned and then donated, the issues involved are similar to those for other sperm or egg donations, except children resulting from multiple cloned eggs or sperms would be more genetically similar than usual egg or sperm donation situations.

Embryo cloning creates embryos that are identical multiples. Using this technology, it would be possible to have identical twins or one child born at one point and another born later (genetic twins that are born years apart). Although identical twins have the same DNA, there are differences between them that stem from their environment. Children created using this method would have identical DNA and thus could not be distinguished using DNA tests. Other identifying features (such as scars or growth differences) would be used to distinguish them, should it ever be necessary. Modern fingerprinting is able to isolate the difference between identical twins most of the time as well.

Somatic nuclear cloning of an adult raises legal issues similar to that of embryo cloning. The child that is born would have identical DNA as its parent, making him an identical twin to the parent. As with embryo cloning though, environment would have an impact on the child and thus he or she could not be exactly the same as the parent and it would be possible to distinguish between them.

Chapter 12

Family Support and Protection

Similar to any other parent, you want to raise your child and focus on your life together. Unfortunately, gay families have to take additional steps to protect themselves and some extra planning is required before you go off into the happily ever after. Take the steps necessary to protect your family, but start focusing on the important job of parenting.

Family Leave

When you add a child to your family, you probably want or need some time off from work either to recover from birth or to adjust to the sudden changes in your life from the addition of a child to your family. There are federal and state laws that allow new parents to take this crucial time off.

The federal Family and Medical Leave Act (FMLA) allows legal parents to take unpaid time off from work to care for a newborn or newly adopted child within the first 12 months after placement of the child, while preserving their jobs. You must work for an employer with at least 50 employees and must have been employed there at least 12 months and worked at least 1,250 hours. You can take up to a total of 12 weeks of leave in a 12-month period. You can take all the leave at once or spread the leave out so that you work some or all of the time on a part-time basis. When possible, you must give 30-days notice of the leave. When you return to work, your employer must reinstate you to your job, or to a similar position.

If your partner is the legal parent and you are not yet a legal parent, you are not eligible to take time off under federal law. However, you have some other options. You could first ask your employer to extend family leave to you because your situation is identical to that of any other parent. You can also arrange to use sick or vacation time, or to take a brief leave without pay. Flex time or job sharing are other options to consider. If you are able to do a same-sex adoption, you would eligible to take time off after the adoption is finalized.

> For more information about FMLA, see *www.dol.gov/ esa/whd/fmla/*.

Some states have family leave laws, so be sure to check with your human resource manager to determine if you are entitled to additional state leave. California has a paid family leave law. You may also qualify for paid maternity or paternity leave or special adoption leave under your company's policies. If you give birth to the child, you will also qualify for disability leave if your state has a disability leave act, or if your company has a disability policy.

Wills and Guardianship

A will is one of the most important tools at your disposal as a parent. A will not only allows you to dispose of your personal property according to your wishes, but it also allows you to choose a guardian for your child should you pass away before the child is an adult. If you are partnered and your partner is not the legal parent of your child, this is the only step you can take to make sure your partner will get custody of your child—and note that the court is not required to follow your request, although most of the time it is honored. Also include an alternate guardian, so that you have a plan in place in case something should happen to both you and your partner. If you are a single parent, or if you and your partner are both legal parents, it is just as important to select a guardian. Talk to the person you think you would prefer to choose and make sure this is something he would be willing to do.

If you are a nonlegal parent, you should specify in your will that you leave your assets to your partner and/or to your children. You can leave your assets to anyone you want, whether you are related to them or not. But if you do not specify this in your will, the state intestacy laws apply and your estate would go to your closest living relatives, not the children you consider to be yours or the partner who is your spouse.

Coparenting Agreements

A coparenting agreement is a written document signed by you and your partner that lays out your intentions to raise your child together. In it you can divide responsibilities and create an agreement for how you would share time with the child should you ever break up. Most of the time, this type of agreement will have no legal enforceability, but it can still be very helpful if you put everything down in writing, so that there can be no future confusion about what you agreed to or what your roles will be. A coparenting agreement can be part of a domestic partnership agreement, and one can also be created with a sperm donor or surrogate to spell out a continuing role in the child's life.

Coparenting agreements have another important function. If you are the legal parent and your partner is not and you die, a coparenting agreement can be used as evidence to help your partner obtain custody of your child. For that reason alone, a coparenting agreement is an important tool.

> For more information visit The National Embryo Donation Center at: *www.embryodonation.org.*

Medical Consents

If you have a partner and she is not a legal parent, you need to execute a consent form that allows him or her to obtain medical care for your child. Contact your pediatrician's office and tell them you want to do this. They will give you the form they prefer to use and keep it in their file. You also need to execute another form that your partner can get to should he need to take the child to the hospital or obtain other emergency care. Don't worry—no ER doctor is going to let your baby bleed to death while your partner digs through her handbag looking for the form. Physicians will do emergency care—to save a life or limb—without parental consent. And often, even if the form can't be located, a telephone call is enough to authorize treatment. But having a consent form done will be a load off of your mind and will make things much easier should medical care ever be needed.

Here is an example of a medical consent form you can prepare yourself:

I,_____, parent of_____,
hereby authorize my partner _____
to make any and all health decisions for my child in
my absence.

_____ _____ _____
Name   Date   Cell phone number

School Consents

Just as only legal parents can make medical decisions, only legal parents can make educational decisions. Schools are used to working with stepparents though and so many do not have a problem with step-parents or others in parental roles picking kids up, attending events, and so on. However, it is a good idea to give the school a written consent form that allows your partner to make decisions about the child, handle phone calls, attend parent-teacher conferences, sign report cards, and so on. Your school probably has a specific form they want you to use, so call and ask.

Health Insurance

In most cases, only a legal parent can put a child on his health insurance plan. If you are adopting a child, you can get him on your plan as soon as he is placed with you for the adoption, before it is finalized. Note however, that the tide is turning about health insurance and now half of all Fortune 500 companies offer health insurance to domestic partners and many (90 percent according to *USA Today*) are now extending that coverage to include dependent children of the domestic partner. Health insurance is an important issue to gay families, because comprehensive coverage of partners and children often means that one partner will be able to stay home with the children, something that would not be possible if he was not covered under his partner's policy.

Other Employment Benefits

Many employers are now offering other family benefits to gay couples and families. Bereavement leave is often extended for the death of a partner's family member or for the death of a partner. Flex time is extended to gay parents who are not legal parents by some employers. Some even provide adoption assistance funding to the domestic partners of employees.

Life Insurance

Life insurance is something you should discuss with your financial advisor. Some experts believe it makes more sense to invest the money you would spend on premiums, but this is an individual decision you need to make. If you are a legal parent, you can take out a life insurance policy and name your child as the beneficiary. However if you are not a legal parent, the child has no insurable interest in your life. It may be possible to name your partner as your beneficiary, and as the guardian of your child. Setting up an investment account is an excellent alternative to life insurance in this kind of situation, and a will allows you to direct the money to your partner without any legal obstacle. Talk to your investment counselor about gifts to minor accounts, joint accounts with right of survivorship, and other options.

Finding Support

There are more and more alternative families and so it is becoming easier to find support. Start on the local level, and find out if there is a local gay families group you could join. Some individual gay and lesbian families work cooperatively so that their children can have close relationships with adults of both sexes. There are also many online groups (see Appendix A) which can offer information and support.

Safe Schools

Once your child is school–aged, you may be concerned about how welcoming the school will be to your family, or how to find a school that will make you feel comfortable. Meet with the principal or another administrator to ask how gay-friendly the school is. Ask the following questions:

- ☑ Does the school provide training to the teachers about GLBT families?

- ☑ Do they have any anti-discrimination employment policies for gays that would indicate a sensitivity to issues of discrimination?

- ☑ Are GLBT issues included in the curriculum at any point or are alternative families discussed?

- ☑ Are school handbooks and applications gender neutral when referring to parents?

- ☑ Are there other GLBT families in the school?

Find out if the school has a gay-straight alliance (GSA), a group that supports students of GLBT families, as well as those older students who are gay themselves. If your school doesn't have one, you can start one. Federal law forbids federally funded schools that allow noncurriculum based groups to meet and use school resources to discriminate about what kind of groups they allow.

Should a problem develop and you feel your child or family is being treated unfairly, contact the Office of Civil Rights with the U.S. Department of Education and file a Title IX complaint. See *www.ed.gov/about/offices/list/ocr/index.html?src=mr* for more information.

> For a list of GLBT-friendly summer camps, visit *www.gayparentmag.com/652295.html*.

Appendix A

Resources

Books

Adamec, Christine. *The Complete Idiot's Guide to Adoption.* New York, N.Y.: Alpha Publishing, 2005.

Barret, Robert. *Gay Fathers: Encouraging the Hearts of Gay Dads and Their Families.* Hoboken, N.J.: Jossey-Bass, 2000.

Brill, Stephanie. *The Queer Parent's Primer: A Lesbian and Gay Families' Guide to Navigating Through a Straight World.* Oakland, CA: New Harbinger Publications, 2001.

Casper, Virginia. *Gay Parents, Straight Schools: Building Communication and Trust.* New York, N.Y.: Teachers College Press, 1999

189

Clunis, Merilee. *The Lesbian Parenting Book*. Emeryville, Calif: Seal Press, 2003.

Erichsen, Jean Nelson and Heino R. Erishsen. *How to Adopt Internationally: A Guide for Agency-Directed and Independent Adoptions*. New York, N.Y.: Mesa House, 2003.

Johnson, Suzanne. *For Lesbian Parents: Your Guide to Helping Your Family Grow Up Happy, Healthy, and Proud*. New York, N.Y.: The Guilford Press, 2001.

Lev, Arlene Istar. *The Complete Lesbian and Gay Parenting Guide*. Lost Angeles, Calif: Berkeley Trade, 2004.

McGarry, Kevin. *Fatherhood for Gay Men: An Emotional and Practical Guide to Becoming a Gay Dad*. San Francisco, Calif: Harrington Park Press, 2003.

Melina, Lois Ruskai. *Open Adoption Experience: Complete Guide for Adoptive and Birth Families*. New York, N.Y.: Harper Paperbacks, 1993.

Mohler, Marie. *A Donor Insemination Guide*. San Francisco, Calif: Harrington Park Press, 2002.

Sember, Brette. *Gay & Lesbian Rights: A Guide for GLBT Singles, Couples, and Families*. Naperville, Ill: Sourcebooks, 2006.

Sember, Brette. *Gay & Lesbian Medical Rights*. Franklin Lakes, N.J.: Career Press, 2006.

Temple-Plotz, Lana. *Practical Tools for Foster Parents*. Lincoln, Nebr.: Boys Town Press, 2002.

Toevs, Kim. *The Essential Guide to Lesbian Conception, Pregnancy, and Birth*. Los Angeles, Calif: Alyson Publications, 2002.

Vercollone, Carol Frost. *Helping the Stork: The Choices and Challenges of Donor Insemination.*. Hoboken, N.J.: Wiley, 1997.

Magazines

And Baby Magazine: *www.andbabymag.com*

Gay Parent Magazine: *www.gayparentmag.com*

Websites

Adoption, General

The Adoption-Friendly Workplaces: *www.adoptionfriendlyworkplace.org/employers.asp*

Adoption Self-Assessment: *http://adoption.about.com*

Domestic vs. International Adoption: *www.adoptall.com/ intguide.html*

Families Like Ours: *www.familieslikeours.org*

Families for Private Adoption: *www.ffpa.org*

Gay Adoption Mailing List: *http://maelstrom.stjohns.edu/ archives gay-aparent.html*

Gay Adoption Support Group: *www.cyberhiway.com/ aparent/faq.html*

National Adoption Foundation: *www.nafadopt.org*

National Adoption Information Clearinghouse: *http://naic.acf.hhs.gov*

National Endowment for Financial Education: *www.nefe.org/adoption/*

National Resource Center for Special Needs Adoption: *www.nrcadoption.org/index.htm*

Open Adoptions: *www.openadoption.org*

Sample Home Study: *www.1-800-homestudy.com/homestudy/sample*

State Adoption Subsidy Profiles: *www.nacac.org subsidy_stateprofiles.html*

State Photo Listings: *www.comeunity.com/adoption/waiting/photolistings.html*

Tuition Waivers and Scholarships for Adopted Children: *www.nacac.org/subsidyfactsheets/tuition.html*

Adoption, International

Choosing an international adoption agency: *www.adopting.org/choosagn.html*

Forms: *http://uscis.gov/graphics/formsfee/forms*

Hague Convention on Intercountry Adoption: *http://uscis.gov/graphics/services/HagueFS.pdf*

International Adoption Consortium: *www.welcomegarden.com/resources_by_state.html*

Joint Council of International Children's Services: *www.jcics.org*

Physicians Who Specialize in Adoption: *www.aap.org/sections/adoption/adopt-states/adoption-map.html*

US Department of State country specific information: *www.travel.state.gov*

Cloning

Clonaid: *www.clonaid.com*

The Human Clone Rights Foundation: *www.humanclonerights.org*

Cryopreservation

American Association of Tissue Banks: *www.aatb.org*

Embryo Donation

Reprotech: *www.reprot.com*

The National Embryo Donation Center: *www.embryodonation.org*

Family Leave

Federal Family and Medical Leave Act: *www.dol.gov/esa/whd/ fmla/*

Foster Care

National Foster Parent Association: *www.nfpainc.org*

The Dave Thomas Foundation for Adoption: *www.DaveThomasFoundationforAdoption.org*

State Foster Care Agencies: *http://foster-parenting.adoption.com/agencies/agencies.php*

State Foster Care Specialists: *www.adopting.org/adoptions/ foster-care-specialists-by-state.html*

Infertility

RESOLVE: *www.resolve.org*

Insurance Laws: *www.asrm.org*

FSAs and procedures: *www.irs.goc/publications/p502/ index.html*

Insemination

Brochure: *www.asrm.org/Literature/patient.html*

Home Insemination:
http:homeinseminations.homestead.com/index.html or
www.fertilityplus.org/faq/homeinsem.html

Legal Information and Assistance

American Academy of Adoption Attorneys:
www.adoptionattorneys.org

Gay & Lesbian Advocates and Defenders: *www.glad.org*

Lambda Legal:*www.lambdalegal.org*

National Center for Lesbian Rights: *www.nclrights.org*

Parenting

And Baby Magazine: *www.andbabymag.com*

Books for Children with GLBT characters:
www.geocities.com

Family Pride Coalition: *www.familypride.org*

Gay Parent Magazine: *www.gayparentmag.com*

Gay Fatherhood: *www.gayfatherhood.com*

Gay Fathers At Home: *www.dadsathome.com*

Our House: a documentary about growing up with gay parents:
www.itvs.org/ourhouse

Proud Parenting: *www.proudparenting.com*

Schools

Gay-Lesbian Straight Education Network: *www.glsen.org*

Office of Civil Rights with the US Department of Education: *www.ed.gov/about/offices/list/ocr/ index.html?src=mr*

Sperm Banks

www.fertilityplus.org/faq/donor.html

Rainbow Flag Health Services: *www.gayspermbank.com*

Surrogacy

Growing Generation: *www.growinggenerations.com*

Sample surrogacy contracts:

www.surrogacy.com/legals/gestcontract.html

www.surromomsonline.com/articles/contract.htm

www.everythingsurrogacy.com/cgi-bin/main.cgi?test

Agencies and Associations

Appendix B

State Adoption Specialists

Alabama Department of Human Resources
Marie Youngpeter
Family Services Partnership, Office of Adoption
50 North Ripley Street
Montgomery, AL 36130-4000
Phone:(334) 242-1374 Fax: (334) 242-0939
E-mail: myoungpeter@dhr.state.al.us
Website: *www.dhr.state.al.us/page.asp?pageid=306*

Alaska Department of Health and Social Services
Linda West
Office of Children's Services
350 Main Street, 4th Floor
PO Box 110630 Juneau, AK 99811-0630
Phone: (907) 465-2145 Fax: (907) 465-3397
E-mail: Linda_west@health.state.ak.us
Website: *www.hss.state.ak.us/ocs/Adoptions/default.htm*

Arizona Department of Economic Security
Angela Cause
Administration for Children, Youth and Families
PO Box 6123 - 940A Phoenix, AZ 85007
Phone: (602) 542-5499 Fax: (602) 542-3330
E-mail: acause@azdes.gov
Website: *www.de.state.az.us/dcyf/adoption/default.asp.*
Spanish Information on Website: *www.de.state.az.us/dcyf/ adoption/spanish.asp*

Arkansas Department of Human Services
Lillie Owens
PO Box 2620
Little Rock, AR 72203
Phone: (501) 682-9273 Fax: (501) 682-9382
E-mail: lillie.owens@arkansas.gov
Website: *www.state.ar.us/dhs/adoption/adoption.html*

California Department of Social Services
Patricia Aguiar Child and Youth Permanency
Branch 744 P Street MS 19-69 Sacramento, CA 95814
Phone: (916) 651-7464 Fax: (916) 324-3044
E-mail: Pat.Aguiar@dss.ca.gov
Website: *www.childsworld.ca.gov/CFSDAdopti_309.htm*

Colorado Department of Human Services (CDHS)
Sharen Ford
1575 Sherman Street 2nd Floor
Denver, CO 80203-1714
Phone: (303) 866-3197 Fax: (303) 866-5563
E-mail: Sharen.Ford@state.co.us
Website: *www.changealifeforever.org/adoption.asp*

Connecticut Department of Children and Families
Office of Foster and Adoption Services
505 Hudson Street
Hartford, CT 06106
Phone: (860) 550-6350 Fax: (860) 556-6726
E-mail: Doreen.Jordan@po.state.ct.us
Website: *www.state.ct.us/dcf/FASU/FASU_index.htm*

Delaware Department of Services for Children, Youth and Their Families (DSCYF)
Frank Perfinski
1825 Faulkland Road
Wilmington, DE 19805
Phone: (302) 633-2655 Fax: (302) 633-2652
E-mail: adoption.dscyf@state.de.us
Website: *www.state.de.us/kids/adoption.htm*

District of Columbia Child and Family Services Agency
400 6th Street SW
Washington, DC 20024
Phone: (202) 727-4733 Fax: (202) 727-7709
E-mail: Wjohnson1@cfsa-dc.org
Website: *http://dhs.dc.gov/dhs/cwp/*
view,a,3,q,492397,dhsNav, |30989|.asp

District of Columbia Child and Family Services Agency
Sharon Knight
400 6th Street SW Room 3042
Washington, DC 20024
Phone: (202) 727-3655 Fax: (202) 727-7709
E-mail: sknight@cfsa-dc.org
Website: *http://dhs.dc.gov/dhs/cwp*

Florida Department of Children and Families
1317 Winewood Boulevard Building 6
Tallahassee, FL 32399-0700
Phone:(850) 922-5055 Fax:(850) 414-8691
E-mail: Kim_Grosdidier@dcf.state.fl.us
Website: *www.dcf.state.fl.us/adoption/*

Georgia Department of Human Resources
Valé Henson
Division of Family and Children Services,
Office of Adoptions
2 Peachtree Street NW Suite 8-400
Atlanta, GA 30303-3142
Phone: (404) 657-3550 Toll-Free: (888) 460-2467
E-mail: vahenson@dhr.state.ga.us
Website: *www.adoptions.dhr.state.ga.us*

Guam Department of Public Health and Social Services
Lydia D. Tenorio
Bureau of Social Services Administration
PO Box 2816
Agana, GU 96910
Phone: (671) 475-2640 Fax: (671) 472-6649
E-mail: lydiat@mail.gov.gu

Hawaii Department of Human Services
Lynne Kazama
810 Richards Street
Suite 400 Honolulu, HI 96813
Phone: (808) 586-5698 Fax: (808) 586-4806
E-mail: lkazama@dhs.hawaii.gov
Website: *www.hawaii.gov/dhs/Media%20Advisory %20Q&A.html*

Idaho Department of Health and Welfare
Susan Dwello
Division of Family and Community Services
450 West State Street, 5th Floor
PO Box 83720
Boise, ID 83720-0036
Phone: (208) 334-5697Fax: (208) 334-6664
E-mail: dwellos@idhw.state.id.us
Website: *www.healthandwelfare.idaho.gov/portal/*

Illinois Department of Children and Family Services
June Dorn
Division of Foster Care and Permanency Services
100 West Randolph Suite 6-100
Chicago, IL 60601
Phone: (312) 814-6858 Fax: (312) 814-8632
E-mail: jdorn@idcfs.state.il.us
Website: *www.state.il.us/dcfs/adoption/index.shtml*

Indiana Division of Family and Children
Department of Child Services
402 West Washington Street Room W392 - MS03
Indianapolis, IN 46204-2739
Phone: (317) 234-3925 Fax: (317) 232-4490
Website: *www.in.gov/fssa/adoption/*

Iowa Department of Human Services—Division of Adult, Children & Family Services (DHS)
Charlcie Carey Hoover
State Office Building, 5th Floor
1305 East Walnut Avenue
Des Moines, IA 50319-0114
Phone: (515) 281-5358 Fax: (515) 242-6036
Toll-Free: (800) 243-0756
E-mail: ccarey@dhs.state.ia.us
Website: *www.dhs.state.ia.us/dhs2005/dhs_homepage/
children_family/adoption/index.html*

Kansas Department of Social and Rehabilitation Services, Children and Family Policy Division
Patricia Long
Docking State Office Building 5th Floor
South 915 SW Harrison, Room 551-S
Topeka, KS 66612-1870
Phone: (785) 296-0918 Fax: (785) 368-8159
E-mail: pal@SRSKANSAS.org
Website: *www.srskansas.org/services/adoption.htm*

Kentucky Department for Community Based Services
Charla Pratt
Cabinet for Families and Children
275 East Main Street 3CE
Frankfort, KY 40621
Phone: (502) 564-2147 Fax: (502) 564-9554
Toll-Free: (800) 232-5437
E-mail: charla.pratt@ky.gov
Website: *http://cfc.state.ky.us/help/adoption.asp*

Louisiana Department of Social Services
Bruce Daniels
Office of Community Services
333 Laurel Street PO Box 3318
Baton Rouge, LA 70821
Phone: (225) 342-4086 Fax: (225) 342-9087
E-mail: bdaniels@dss.state.la.us
Website:*www.dss.state.la.us/departments/ocs/*
Adoption_Services.html

Maine Department of Health and Human Services
Virginia Marriner Bureau of Child and Family Services
221 State Street State House Station #11
Augusta, ME 04333-0011
Phone: (207) 287-5060 (207) 287-2976 Fax: (207) 287-5282
TDD:(207) 287-5048
E-mail: Virginia.s.marriner@maine.gov
Website: *www.afamilyforme.org/adopt.html*

Maryland Department of Human Resources
Stephanie Pettaway
311 West Saratoga Street
Baltimore, MD 21201
Phone: (410) 767-7506 Fax: (410) 333-0922
E-mail: spettawa@dhr.state.md.us
Website: *www.dhr.state.md.us/ssa/adopt.htm*

Massachusetts Department of Social Services
Leo Farley
24 Farnsworth Street
Boston, MA 02210
Phone: (617) 748-2267 Fax: (617) 261-7437
Website: *www.mass.gov/portal*

Michigan Department of Human Services
Kate Hanley Child and Family Services Administration
PO Box 30037 Suite 413
Lansing, MI 48909
Phone:(517) 373-3513 Fax:(517) 335-4019
E-mail: hanleyk@michigan.gov
Website: *www.michigan.gov/fia/14-5452_7116—,00.html*

Minnesota Department of Human Services
Connie Caron
Human Services Building
444 Lafayette Road
St. Paul, MN 55155-3831
Phone: (651) 282-3793 Fax: (651) 297-1949
E-mail: connie.caron@state.mn.us
Website: *www.dhs.state.mn.us*

Mississippi Department of Human Services
Phoebe Clark
Division of Family and Child Services
750 North State Street
Jackson, MS 39202
Phone: (601) 359-4981 Fax: (601) 359-4226
E-mail: pclark@mdhs.state.ms.us
Website: *www.mdhs.state.ms.us/fcs_adopt.html*

Missouri Department of Social Services
Cindy Wilkinson
Children's Division
615 Howerton Court PO Box 88
Jefferson City, MO 65103-0088
Phone: (573) 751-3171 Fax: (573) 526-3971
E-mail: cindy.r.wilkinson@dss.mo.gov
Website: *www.dss.mo.gov/cd/adopt.htm*

Montana Department of Public Health and Human Services
Child and Family Services Division
P.O. Box 8005 Helena, MT 59604
Phone: (406) 444-5919
E-mail: lkorth@mt.gov
Website: *www.dphhs.state.mt.us/aboutus/divisions/*
childfamilyservices/adoption/adoptioninmontana.shtml

Nebraska Department of Health and Human Services
Mary Dyer
P.O. Box 95044
301 Centennial Mall South Child and Family Services Division
Lincoln, NE 68509-5044
Phone: (402) 471-9331 Fax: (402) 471-9034
E-mail: mary.dyer@hhss.ne.gov
Website: *www.hhs.state.ne.us/chs/adp/adpindex.htm*

Nevada Department of Human Resources
Wanda Scott
Division of Child and Family Services
4220 South Maryland Parkway Building B, Suite 300
Las Vegas, NV 89119
Phone: (702) 486-7633 Fax: (702) 486-7626
E-mail: wlscott@dcfs.state.nv.us
Website: *http://dcfs.state.nv.us/page33.html*

New Hampshire Department of Health and Human Services
Cathernie Atkins
Division for Children, Youth and Families
129 Pleasant Street Brown Building
Concord, NH 03301
Phone: (603) 271-4707 Fax: (603) 271-4729
E-mail: catkins@dhhs.state.nh.us
Website: *www.dhhs.state.nh.us*

New Jersey Department of Human Services—Division of Youth and Family Services
Daryl Bender
Office of Adoption Operations
P.O. Box 717
Trenton, NJ 08625
Phone: (609) 984-6080 Fax: (609) 984-5449
E-mail: Daryl.Bender@dhs.state.nj.us
Website: *www.state.nj.us*

New Mexico Department of Children, Youth and Families
Mark Ruttkay
PERA Building, Room 254
P.O. Drawer 5160
Santa Fe, NM 87502-5160
Phone: (505) 827-8400 Fax: (505) 827-8480
E-mail: mjruttkay@cyfd.state.nm.us
Website: *www.cyfd.org/index.htm*

New York State Office of Children and Family Services/ Adoption Service (OCFS/NYSAS)
Lee Lounsbury
Office of Children and Family Services
52 Washington Street Room 323
North Rensselaer, NY 12144
Phone: (518) 474-9406 Fax: (518) 486-6326
Toll-Free: (800) 345-5437
E-mail: lee.lounsbury@dfa.state.ny.us
Website: *www.ocfs.state.ny.us/adopt*

North Carolina Department of Health and Human Services
Esther High
Division of Social Services
325 North Salisbury Street

2409 Mail Service Center
Raleigh, NC 27699-2409
Phone: (919) 733-9464 Fax: (919) 733-3052
E-mail: esther.high@ncmail.net
Website: *www.dhhs.state.nc.us/dss/adopt/*

North Dakota Department of Human Services (NDDHS)
Julie Hoffman
Children and Family Services Division
State Capitol, Department 325
Bismarck, ND 58505
Phone: (701) 328-4805 Fax: (701) 328-3538
Toll-Free: (800) 245-3736
E-mail: sohofj@state.nd.us
Website: *www.state.nd.us/humanservices/services/*
childfamily/adoption/

Ohio Department of Job and Family Services
Barbara Harris
Office of Family and Child Services
255 East Main Street 3rd Floor
Columbus, OH 43215
Phone: (614) 466-9274 Fax: (614) 728-2604
E-mail: harrib06@odjfs.state.oh.us
Website: *http://jfs.ohio.gov/oapl/index.htm*

Oklahoma Department of Human Services
Children & Family Services Division
P.O. Box 25352
Oklahoma City, OK 73125
Phone: (405) 522-2467 Fax: (405) 521-2433
E-mail: Margaret.Devault@okdhs.org
Website: *www.okdhs.org/adopt*

Oklahoma Department of Human Services
Deborah Goodman
Adoption Services
907 South Detroit Suite 750
Tulsa, OK 74120
Phone: (405) 521-2475 Fax: (918) 592-9149
E-mail: Deborah.Goodman@okdhs.org
Website: *www.okdhs.org/adopt*

Oregon Department of Human Services
Office of Permanency for Children and of Training
Kathy Ledesma
Human Services Building, Adoption Unit, 2nd Floor
500 Summer Street NE, E-71 Salem, OR 97310-1068
Phone: (503) 945-5677 Fax: (503) 945-6969
E-mail: kathy.ledesma@state.or.us
Website: *www.dhs.state.or.us/children/adoption/*

Pennsylvania Department of Public Welfare
Tina Weber
Office of Children, Youth and Families
P.O. Box 2675
Harrisburg, PA 17105
Phone: (717) 783-7287 Fax: (717) 346-9663
E-mail: chweber@state.pa.us
Website: *www.dpw.state.pa.us/Child/AdoptionFosterCare/*
003670363.htm

Puerto Rico Department of Family
P.O. Box 194090
San Juan, PR 00959-4090

Phone: (787) 773-0936 Fax: (787) 773-0943
E-mail: cnazarioadfan@yahoo.com
Website: *http://serviciosenlinea.gobierno.pr/CitizenPortal/*
123-004-006-000.htm

Rhode Island Department of Children, Youth and Families
Maureen Robbins
Adoption & Foster Care Preparation & Support
101 Friendship Street 3rd Floor Providence, RI 02903
Phone: (401) 528-3799 Fax: (401) 528-3870
E-mail: maureen.robbins@dcyf.ri.gov
Website: *www.dcyf.ri.gov/adoption.htm*

South Carolina Department of Social Services
Carolyn Orf
Office of Program Policy and Oversight
1535 Confederate Avenue Columbia, SC 29202
Phone: (803) 898-7707 Fax: (803) 898-7792
E-mail: corf@dss.state.sc.us
Website: *www.state.sc.us/dss/adoption/index.html*

South Dakota Department of Social Services
Patricia Reiss
Department of Child Protective Services
700 Governor's Drive
Pierre, SD 57501-2291
Phone: (605) 773-3227 Fax: (605) 773-6834
E-mail: patricia.reiss@state.sd.us
Website: *www.state.sd.us/social/cps/adoption/index.htm*

Tennessee Department of Children's Services
Mattie Satterfield
Cordell Hull Building, 8th Floor 436
Sixth Avenue North Nashville, TN 37243-1290
Phone: (615) 532-5637 Fax: (615) 532-6495
E-mail: mattie.satterfield@state.tn.us
Website: *www.state.tn.us/youth/foster/index.htm*

Texas Department of Family and Protective Services
701 West 51st Street PO Box 149030, Mail Code E-558
Austin, TX 78714-9030
Phone: (512) 438-3412 Fax: (512) 438-3782
E-mail: janis.brown@dfps.state.tx.us
Website: *www.tdprs.state.tx.us/Adoption_and_*
Foster_Care/About_Adoption/default.asp

Utah Department of Human Services
Marty Shannon
Division of Child and Family Services
12 North 200 West, Suite 225
Salt Lake City, UT 84103
Phone: (801) 538-3913 Fax: (801) 538-3993
E-mail: mshannon@utah.gov
Website: *www.hsdcfs.utah.gov/adoption.htm*

Vermont Department of Social and Rehabilitation Services
Diane Dexter
Division of Social Services
103 South Main Street
Waterbury, VT 05671
Phone: (802) 241-2142 Fax: (802) 241-2407
E-mail: ddexter@srs.state.vt.us
Website: *www.path.state.vt.us/cwyj/adoption/*

Virgin Islands Department of Human Services
Etta Rahming
1303 Hospital Ground Building A-Knud Hansen Complex
St. Thomas, VI 00802
Phone: (340) 774-0930, ext. 4243 Fax: (340) 774-0082
E-mail: erahming@hotmail.com

Virginia Department Of Social Services
Brenda Kerr
7 North 8th Street
Richmond, VA 23219
Phone: (804) 726-7530 Fax: (804) 726-7499
Toll-Free:(888) 821-HOPE (4673)
E-mail: brenda.kerr@dss.virginia.gov
Website: *www.dss.virginia.gov/family/ap/index.html*

Washington Department of Social and Health Services
Pam Kramer Division of Children and Family Services
1115 Washington Street, SE PO Box 45713
Olympia, WA 98504
Phone: (360) 902-7968 Fax: (360) 902-7903
E-mail: caip300@dshs.wa.gov
Website: *www1.dshs.wa.gov/ca/adopt/intro.asp*

West Virginia Department of Health and Human Resources
Laura Lou Harbert Office of Social Services
Children and Adult Services
350 Capitol Street, Room 691
Charleston, WV 25301
Phone: (304) 558-4303 Fax: (304) 558-4563
E-mail: lauraharbert@wvdhhr.org
Website: *www.wvdhhr.org/oss/adoption/*

Wisconsin Department of Health and Family Services
Dale Langer
Division of Child and Family Services
1 West Wilson, Room 527 PO Box 8916
Madison, WI 53707-8916
Phone: (608) 266-3595 Fax: (608) 264-6750
E-mail: langedw@dhfs.state.wi.us
Website: *www.dhfs.state.wi.us/children/adoption/index.htm*

Wyoming Department of Family Services
Maureen Clifton
130 Hobbs Avenue
Cheyenne, WY 82009
Phone: (307) 777-3570 Fax: (307) 777-3693
E-mail: mclift@state.wy.us
Website: *http://dfsweb.state.wy.us/adoption.html*

State Photolisting Websites

Alaska Adoption Exchange
www.akae.org/

Arkansas Adoption Resource Exchange
www.accessarkansas.org/dhs/adoption/adoption.html

Arizona Department of Economic Security
www.de.state.az.us/dcyf/adoption/meet.asp

California Kids Connection
www.CAKidsConnection.com

Colorado: The Adoption Exchange
www.adoptex.org

Connecticut Department of Children and Families
www.adoptuskids.org/states/ct/

Delaware: Adoption Center of Delaware Valley
www.acdv.org/waiting_children.html

Florida Department of Children and Families
www.dcf.state.fl.us/adoption/

Georgia: My Turn Now Photolisting
http://167.193.144.179/mtnmenu2.asp

Iowa: KidSake Foster/Adopt Iowa
www.iakids.org

Illinois: Adoption Information Center of Illinois (AICI)
www.adoptinfo-il.org

Indiana Adoption Resource Network
www.in.gov/dcs/adoption/

Kentucky: Special Needs Adoption Program (SNAP)
http://apps.chfs.ky.gov/snap/

Louisiana Adoption Resource Exchange (LARE)
www.adoptuskids.org/states/la

Massachusetts Adoption Resource Exchange, Inc.
www.mareinc.org

Maryland Adoption Resource Exchange (MARE)
www.adoptuskids.org/states/md/

Michigan Adoption Resource Exchange (MARE)
www.mare.org

Minnesota Adoption Resource Network, Inc.
www.mnadopt.org/

Missouri Adoption Photolisting
www.adoptuskids.org

Mississippi Adoption Resource Exchange
www.mdhs.state.ms.us/fcs_adopt.html#children

Montana Department of Public Health and Human Services
www.dphhs.mt.gov/aboutus/divisions/childfamilyservices/
adoption/adoptioninmontana.shtml

Montana Waiting Children Photolistings
www.adoptuskids.org/states/mt

North Carolina Kids Adoption and Foster Care Network
www.adoptuskids.org/states/nc/

North Dakota Department of Human Services (NDDHS)
www.state.nd.us/humanservices/services/childfamily/adop
tion/adoptuskids.html

New Hampshire Department of Health and Human Services
www.dhhs.state.nh.us/DHHS/FCADOPTION/default.htm

New Jersey Youth and Family Services Adoption Exchange
www.state.nj.us/humanservices/adoption/childframe.html

New Mexico Department of Children, Youth and Families
www.cyfd.org/index.htm

Nevada Photolisting Service
http://dcfs.state.nv.us/

New York State Office of Children and Family Services
www.ocfs.state.ny.us/adopt

Ohio: AdoptOHIO
www.odjfs.state.oh.us

Oregon's Waiting Children
www.nwae.org/wait-or.html

Pennsylvania Adoption Exchange (PAE)
www.adoptpakids.org/

Rhode Island: Adoption Rhode Island
www.adoptionri.org/

South Carolina Council on Adoptable Children
www.sc-adopt.org/

Texas Adoption Resource Exchange (TARE)
www.adoptchildren.org

Utah Adoption Exchange
www.utdcfsadopt.org/

Virginia: Adoption Resource Exchange of Virginia (AREVA)
www.adoptuskids.org/states/va

Vermont's Waiting Children
www.projectfamily.state.vt.us/meetTheKids.html

Washington Adoption Resource Exchange (WARE)
www.warekids.org

West Virginia Adoption Resource Network
www.wvdhhr.org/oss/adoption/

Wyoming Department of Family Services
http://dfsweb.state.wy.us/adoption.html

Index

About the Author

Brette McWhorter Sember is a former family law attorney and mediator. She is the author of *Gay & Lesbian Rights: A Guide for GLBT Singles, Couples, and Families* (Sourcebooks, 2006), *The Complete Gay Divorce* (Career Press, 2005), *The Infertility Answer Book* (Sourcebooks, 2005), *Your Practical Pregnancy Planner: Everything You Need to Know About the Financial and Legal Aspects of Preparing for Your New Baby* (McGraw-Hill, 2005), and *Your Plus-Size Pregnancy: The Ultimate Guide for Full-Figured Expectant Moms* (Barricade Books, 2005).